The Bare Bones Biz Plan

Six Weeks to an Extraordinary Business

ELLEN ROHR

www.BareBonesBiz.com
877.629.7647

This book is intended as a reference volume only, and the material enclosed is designed to help you make sound financial decisions about your business, but it is not intended as a substitute for professional, legal, or business advice.

Bare Bones Business Books may be purchased for business or promotional use or for special sales. For sales information or permissions to reprint the this text or the material within, contact the publisher at:

Bare Bones Business Publishing
3120 S. Know It All Lane
Rogersville, MO 65472
877.629.7647

www.barebonesbiz.com

ISBN 13: 978-0-9845876-1-2

Printed in the U.S.A.

Contents

Welcome to the Bare Bones Biz Plan!

Just getting started in business? Great! I'll help you visualize your ideal business and create a solid plan for making it happen. Good for you for planning ahead.

However, most business owners jump head first into business...*then* realize that a plan would be a good idea.

Is that you? Are you in business already, but drowning in the day-to-day problems? I can help you, too. This book can help fix your most pressing problems...and craft a strategy for moving forward. Are you growing too fast...or not fast enough? I have special tips for using this plan to create and handle fast, profitable growth.

The Bare Bones Biz Plan offers a simple strategy for creating a business plan and *using it* to build an extraordinary business. All you need is yourself and a three-ring binder. Commit to 60 minutes a day, five days a week, over the course of six weeks. I'll help you create your Bare Bones Biz Plan Binder, a workable plan for crafting your Vision and making it happen.

Follow the steps in this easy-to-use book, and you will have your plan for creating and expanding your business. You can become physically fit with a sound diet and exercise. *The Bare Bones Biz Plan* uses this time-tested approach to help you become fiscally fit. *The Bare Bones Biz Plan* works!

The Bare Bones Biz Plan is...

- **REAL!** Lots of business books tell you WHAT to do. Like, "Be sure to create a budget." Or, "Look at your financials." (What does THAT mean?) I tell you HOW and I show you...step by step.
- **STRAIGHTFORWARD!** It's about the money, honey! Bare Bones Businesses are "open book" companies. You'll learn how to keep score in the game of business...and share that vital information with your

team. You'll drag "the books" out of the dark and into the Plan Binder.

- BUSINESS BUILDING! As you fill in the pages in the Plan Binder, you can share them with your banker, your employees, your spouse, or potential investors to gather financial and emotional support.

Each week you'll handle one of the six main areas of business and build your Bare Bones Business Plan Binder: *Setting Sight*, *Building the Team*, *Making Money*, *Getting it Sold*, *Getting it Done* and *Making Sure*.

I'll share success stories and give examples of what not to do! I'll include forms, tools and checklists for making business easy and profitable. And I'll help you get and stay organized. Each week's lesson will build on the week before.

It's all about achieving freedom. Freedom from stress and worry. Financial freedom. *The Bare Bones Biz Plan* can help you achieve true freedom...Help you be free to live the life you want to live.

Note: For more help building your business, check out www.BareBonesBiz.com.

All you need are six weeks and a three-ring binder to build an extraordinary business!

The Bare Bones Biz Team
info@barebonesbiz.com
www.barebonesbiz.com
877.629.7647
417.753.3685 fax
3120 S. Know It All Lane
Rogersville, MO 65742
I wish you love, peace and lots of money!

Why I Wrote This Book

With hope in your heart, you hang out your shingle and become a business owner. (Author Michael Gerber calls this an "entrepreneurial seizure.") Then, the day-to-day burdens of running the business take over. Errands, bills, phone calls, and of course, the actual work. Inside each small business owner is the unspoken question, "What am I doing?"

Or you long to start a business and free yourself from the limitations of a corporate job that doesn't match your needs or wants or reflect your values. But you wonder, "Where do I start?"

It's no wonder you are frustrated. Business basics are just not taught—even in business school or by well-meaning business-book authors. Most business education focuses on philosophy and platitudes instead of meat-and-potatoes HOW TO.

I aim to change that. Picture a world transformed by sane and profitable small businesses. Business literacy is empowering and equalizing. Do what you love, make lots of money, spread it around, energize other people and projects... What a wonderful economic vision!

However, if business owners don't get profitable, they will have traded in their corporate salaries, benefits and pensions for a nightmare of debt and endless working hours.

Going out of business is not the worst thing that can happen. Staying in a losing business is much worse. How terrible to be afraid to close the doors because bankruptcy will come knocking. How saddening to have talked your spouse into extending the second mortgage to keep your dream alive, then realizing you aren't going to be able to make the payment...again.

I don't want that to happen to you.

My Mission: Achieving Freedom. Your own extraordinary business is a path to peace, prosperity and freedom across the universe.

Together, we can create honorable, profitable free trade. We can promote World Peace. That's what your extraordinary business can do.

That's why I wrote this book and created www.barebonesbiz.com. I've helped lots of folks move from out-of-luck to big bucks by assembling a Binder just like the one in this plan. The key is to craft the Vision and the Plan...then USE them to help you stay on track. *The Bare Bones Biz Plan* is simple, real, portable...essential to your success. It's all about helping you make a living doing what you love and affecting the planet in a powerful, positive way.

All you need are Six Weeks and a Three-Ring Binder to build a better business!

Today you start on a grand adventure. You are going to build a business...one that works. One that makes money. One that enhances your life. You are going to build a business that only YOU can build, reflecting your unique gifts, talents, dreams and ambitions.

So...Ready, Set...Let's GO!

Instructions for The Bare Bones Biz Plan

Over the next six weeks, this book will take you through the process of creating your business plan. The process is called *The Bare Bones Biz Plan.* The end result is a three-ring Binder, your Bare Bones Biz Plan Binder, and in it will be YOUR customized plan for creating and growing a profitable, successful business. Over the next six weeks, we are going to get your business whipped into shape!

This book addresses one main area of your business each week for six weeks.

- **Week One:** *Setting Sight* – What does it look like when you're done? How will you know when you've "made it"?
- **Week Two**: Building the Team – Who does what? Why, how and when? Put together an unstoppable team.
- **Week Three:** Making Money – Bare-Bones Basics will help you build a budget, keep score and bring in big bucks.
- **Week Four:** Getting it Sold – Sell without insulting your soul.
- **Week Five**: Getting it Done – Use my sure-fire systems for delivering on your promises.
- **Week Six:** Making Sure – Are you on the right track? Are you delivering what people want? Implement my no-hassle quality assurance systems.

Each week, you'll find a coaching lesson plus five assignments—one each for Monday through Friday. Can you spend an hour a day on your business? Sure! But don't beat yourself up if you miss a day or if you take longer to complete the assignments. Set your own pace. Commit to at least one focused hour every day. Do the exercises quickly, and trust your initial thoughts and ideas. Every effort you make to improve your business–and your life–will create positive results. Just keep moving forward!

Skim through each week ahead of time. Block out the time needed to do the exercises in your Day Planner or other calendar. Some exercises require help from team members. Plan ahead accordingly. (I have good suggestions for helping you get organized in the *Getting it Done* section.)

Each week wraps up with an easy weekend assignment that helps you "soak in" what you have learned and apply it. What works, works in all areas of your life. As your business improves, so will other aspects of your life.

I'll provide sample forms. For examples, I'll use See More Blinds and Window Coverings, Inc., a company that provides beautiful window coverings for its customers' delight and privacy. Owner Ted and his team will demonstrate how to use some of the forms.

Here's what you'll need to build your Bare Bones Biz Plan Binder…

- A two-inch, three-ring Binder
- A set of Binder tabs…the kind with eight tabs that you can customize with your computer
- A computer. If you don't have one, borrow one or use one at a local school or library.

And I am here to help every step of the way. I have downloadable, customizable forms, checklists and programs that support this book and can help you create your plan. Check out the Buy Stuff page at www.barebonesbiz.com.

If you are contemplating more than one business idea, create a Plan Binder for each one. The process will help you decide which one to energize and which to ignore (or energize later).

The Binder Tabs

As you set up your Plan Binder, you have tabs for the six areas of your business: *Setting Sight, Building the Team, Making Money, Getting it Sold, Getting it Done*, and *Making Sure.*

Work your way through *The Bare Bones Biz Plan*. Day by day, week by week, you will learn how to build each area of your business. Store your work in each section under the corresponding Binder tab.

The two additional tabs are for the *Master To-Do List* and your *Journal.*

The Master To-Do List

You are going to have lots of great ideas for your business, but you can't do everything all at once. You will learn to prioritize your ideas and focus your energy on the things that will have the most impact on your business success. The Master To-Do List is where you store those ideas. I have it organized into sections that correspond to the six areas of your business: *Setting Sight, Building the Team, Making Money, Getting it Sold, Getting it Done* and *Making Sure.*

When you have a good idea (or a team member does) or you think of something that needs to be done, a "to do"…jot it down on the Master To-Do List. Find the Master To-Do List form at the end of this section. You can also use a simple, single subject spiral notebook for your Master To-Do List. (That's what I use.)

The Journal

This is where you write down the story of your business. You can use the Word document and type out your thoughts. Or print up a few blank Journal pages and store them in the Journal section of your Plan Binder. Then use those pages to write down your…

- Thoughts
- Feelings
- Frustrations
- Wins, losses
- Problems, discovered solutions
- Milestones
- Burning questions
- What happened, why?
- What didn't happen, why not?
- Prayers, moments of epiphany

Date your entries. You will learn wonderful lessons from *The Bare Bones Biz Plan*...and from conceiving and creating your business plan. Keeping a Journal will help you to remember those lessons and give you a nice way to pass the lessons along.

Building the Plan Binder

After you read each day's coaching lesson, copy the forms and checklists from the book and complete the exercises. Or visit www.barebonesbiz.com and download the forms and checklists. Customize them. Print them. And put the customized pages in your Plan Binder...in the appropriate sections, divided by the Binder Tabs.

This is how you create your Bare Bones Biz Plan Binder, your business plan for discovering your entrepreneurial dream and turning it into reality.

If you like, you can build an electronic version of your Bare Bones Biz Plan Binder on your computer.

Still, a two-inch, three-ring Binder is a wonderful thing. I recommend printing your pages and inserting them in your Plan Binder, using the tabs to keep the sections organized. When you update a file, rip out the old version and insert the new one. The Plan Binder is portable. It's easy to access the information you want in the Plan Binder. You're more likely to use *The Bare Bones Biz Plan* in Binder form. Also, it is easier for you to show someone your plan in the Plan Binder than on the computer screen.

Build a Better Business...in Six Weeks

At the end of six weeks, you'll have your Bare Bones Biz Plan Binder–your living, breathing plan for making your business dreams come true. And your business will be glowing with the results of the time and energy you invest in this Biz program. Just like physical fitness, the process requires an ongoing effort. *The Bare Bones Biz Plan* will give your business a jump-start. The Maintenance Plan at the end of the book will help you keep the momentum going.

Commit!

Decide now that you will honor your dreams and allow yourself to be successful. "I commit to learning and doing. I choose to spend at least one hour a day, five days a week, for six weeks, thinking about and working on my business. I promise to complete *The Bare Bones Biz Plan* to the best of my ability. I promise to discover my highest purpose and claim it."

Signed: ____

Date: ____________________

Sample Document Master To-Do List

Updated____________________

This list is the storage place for all ideas, to do's and projects that are as yet unassigned. If any team member has an idea for bettering any aspect of the company, store it here in the appropriate division. This way, all good ideas are in one spot, waiting to be assigned and accomplished.

SETTING SIGHT

- ☐
- ☐

MAKING MONEY

- ☐
- ☐

BUILDING THE TEAM

- ☐
- ☐

GETTING IT SOLD

- ☐
- ☐

GETTING IT DONE

- ☐
- ☐

MAKING SURE

- ☐
- ☐

Sample Document Journal

Updated___________________

Keep a Journal of your journey. You will learn valuable lessons along the path of building your business. You'll need to vent your frustrations. You'll want to remember the funny things that happen. Here's the place to write down the story of your adventure. Use as many pages as you need.

Don't judge anything you write, just write. This is for your eyes only, unless you choose to share all or part of it. As you become more and more successful, these entries may become more valuable to someone else who wants to travel the better-business road.

www.BareBonesBiz.com
877.629.7647

Day ONE

Monday's Coaching Lession: What Do You Want?

"When you determine what you want, you have made the most important decision of your life. You have to know what you want in order to attain it."
~ Douglas Lurton

The Bare Bones Biz Plan will show you how to build a successful business. And if your business falls short of your wildest dreams, there are only two possible reasons:

1. You are neglecting to do the Bare Bones Basics that make all the difference to your success.
2. You are not clear on what you want.

We are living in a Renaissance age. This is a shining period of opportunity, creation and invention.

> *"Never at any time in the past have man's opportunities been so abundant as they are today. We hear people say that all the opportunities that are worth anything have been found and used. This is not so. Opportunities are born in the brain. As the brainpower increases opportunities increase, and the most casual survey of the world's intellectual record will prove that the tide of human thought is on the rise. Never before has education been so widely diffused as it is today; and never before has it been so proud and comprehensive. Never before has invention been so prolific and so wonderfully fruitful. Never before has art and science been so fecund, and never before has the world had so many capable minds at work delving so deeply to find out and apply the basic laws of Nature for the betterment of human life. The man who criticizes and finds fault with the opportunities of today is blind to the advancement and progress going on around him."*

This is as true today as it was in 1916, when business author Albert J. Hall made the observation in his powerful book, *Why Men Fail.* You are not at the mercy of the economy, or the environment, or your family, or your boss…or any other external force. You are responsible for your success. And now is the best time to claim it.

To succeed, you will need to take responsibility for your choices and your actions. From this point forward, you are forbidden to lay blame on anyone or anything for your failures so far and for the mistakes you are bound to make.

Quit whining. Acknowledge your fears and resolve to be successful anyway. You have only ONE problem. The problem is YOU. You keep getting in your own way. The cool thing is that you can change that. You can transform yourself and your business. You are entitled to success. It's up to you to resolve the two issues that are keeping you from being a winner in business...and in life. *The Bare Bones Biz Plan* can help you do that.

This week, you will assemble the *Setting Sight* section of your Plan Binder. You may want to work through the *Setting Sight* exercises by yourself. Or you may want to include one or two others who are involved or whom you intend to involve in the business. Ultimately, one person...YOU...will sign off on the direction of the company. While a great business is the result of a team effort, it is born of one person's intention. The direction of the company is YOUR responsibility.

The first assignment is just for you. Today's assignment is to determine what you want, determine what your purpose is and how your business can help you manifest that.

Let's start with what you *want*...

Perfect Life Exercise

Yes, this is a book for planning a business. However, the reality is that there is NO separation between business and the rest of your life. Your business is an aspect of your life and needs to align with your highest wants and purposes.

What you want is the key to discovering your purpose in life. Sure, you want more... or enough...or something different from what you now have. But be more specific. What exactly do you want?

Write down your Perfect Life. Take a deep breath. Let it out...and calm your mind. Then ask yourself, "What do I want?" and listen for the very first thoughts that come to mind. Write them down without judgment. Notice your feelings as you write the words on the Perfect Life form. If it feels good, you are on the right track.

Use the page in this book titled "Perfect Life." Or you can create a Word® document. You can also find forms and spreadsheets in the Buy Stuff page at www.BareBonesBiz.com. Start with when you wake up, and move through each hour of the day. Jot down thoughts and descriptions of what the Perfect Life would be like. How would you spend it? With whom? Where? Would you work? What does your company look like? How many people? How much money would you make? How much time would you spend with your family?

Contemplate how a business fits into your Perfect Life. What does it look like, smell like, feel like? What kind of work do you do? Who are your customers? How much time would you spend in your business? What hours would you work, ideally? Write it down. Find pictures that capture how you see this business. Incorporate business elements into your Perfect Life.

Write it all down. Add the picture pages. This is your Perfect Life. Store your Perfect Life in your Bare Bones Biz Plan Binder under the *Setting Sight* tab.

List of Spiritual Resources

This is a deeply spiritual exercise. You might need some spiritual guidance. Enjoy reading and learning from these books…

- *The Power of Intention* by Dr. Wayne Dyer
- *The Way to Happiness* by L. Ron Hubbard
- *The Day that Turns Your Life Around* by Jim Rohn
- *The One-Minute Millionaire* by Mark Victor Hansen and Robert G. Allen
- *Creating Affluence* by Deepak Chopra
- *Mastery* by George Leonard
- The Bible
- *The Law of Attraction* by Esther and Jerry Hicks
- *The Power of Now* by Eckhart Tolle

Spend up to an hour on this exercise today. You will come back to it, and you can add to it or revise it as your understanding of your wants and desires gains clarity. This exercise may come easily to you, or you may find this the most challenging work you have ever done. Seek to find your authentic desires. Honor that which you want, because your unique gifts and talents are found there. Relax in the understanding that when you focus on these gifts and talents, you will find ways to share them. Therein lies your purpose.

When you are finished, read what you wrote and look over the pictures. Then give thanks that these things are manifesting for you.

Find Inspiration Anywhere

For inspiration for your Perfect Life exercise, you may want to go to a bookstore. Visit the magazine rack. Buy a dozen magazines specializing in the kinds of things and activities that inspire you. Check out the travel section of the store. Buy a book about a place you want to visit or a map of a place you want to live. You can also search the Internet and print out pictures and pages of things you want to have and things you want to do. Pay attention to what inspires you, to what makes your heart beat faster.

Take pictures of things or activities that inspire you. If you see a garden, or a car, or a pair of shoes that pleases you, take a picture. Clip inspiring articles from the newspaper. Find brochures for your ideal home, office, vacation, software program, community service program, etc. Find pictures that capture what you want from relationships, personal and professional. Discover words and images that stir you on a spiritual level. With a glue stick, scissors and some blank paper, create pages that describe what you really want.

Sample Document Perfect Life Exercise

Updated____________________

Be specific: Who, what, where, when, how? Use numbers, dollars, percentages, names, places. Incorporate all aspects of your life…spiritual, family and relationships, financial, professional, lifestyle. Use ALL FIVE SENSES! Have fun…DREAM…and write down your Perfect Life.

I wake up...

...and then I go to sleep.

Day TWO

Tuesday's Coaching Lesson: What's the Point and Who Benefits?

"Everything you want is out there waiting for you to ask. Everything you want also wants you. But you have to take action to get it."
~ Jack Canfield

Whether you are just starting your business or you are in business already, you need to ask...and answer...these questions:

- Does your business serve you?
- Does it move you toward your Perfect Life?
- What's the point?
- Why should this business exist?
- Who benefits from this business?

Today's first exercise is to craft a Mission Statement...a brief explanation of WHY your business exists. Then you'll define your Target Market...those who can benefit by doing business with you.

Why should this business exist?

If the WHY is big enough, it will give you the courage and strength to follow through with your business plan. It will also provide support for *Building the Team*, *Making Money*, *Getting it Sold*, *Getting it Done* and *Making Sure*. Your Mission Statement is the cornerstone of your business.

Tom Chappell of Tom's Of Maine started his natural grooming-products company in 1970. The Mission: To form a company that would be kind to man and nature. Since then, he and his wife Kate have grown the company to nearly $30 million in annual sales. Tom's top products: natural toothpastes and phosphate-free soaps. In 1986, Tom had a mid-life crisis. Having made a fortune selling soap and toothpaste, he was looking for more meaning. He enrolled in Harvard University's Harvard Divinity School, where he studied scriptures and philosophy. His spiritual awakening? A new Mission: To make the business a ministry. The Mission evolved.

Note that profits are essential to Tom's ministry. Ten percent of pretax profits go to good causes selected by his employees. So the more profit they make, the more they can contribute.

Mission Statement Exercise

Now it's your turn. Find inspiration in your Perfect Life exercise. Also consider the BIG IDEA or moment of epiphany that may have caused you to start your business.

Spend time thinking about WHY you are in business. Too often, the day-to-day demands on our time and energy keep us from thinking about the things that really matter. When you are thinking, it doesn't look like you are doing anything! Rest assured that thinking is the highest-level work you can do.

Ask these questions, think, and write down your thoughts...

- Why should my business exist?
- What excites me about it?
- How does my company impact people, communities, countries, and the planet?
- What would be lost without my business?
- What would be gained without my business?
- What inspired me to start my business?
- What's the point?

Distill the thoughts you have written until you can summarize your Mission Statement in eight seconds or less. Keep it simple and focused. Read your Mission Statement out loud several times a day and commit it to memory.

Don't worry about coming up with the right Mission Statement. Trust that by asking these questions, you will discover your Mission. *The Bare Bones Biz Plan* is a flexible, living, growing plan. As you grow and change, you can come back to this page and revise and refine your Mission. Put down what rings true for you now.

Your next exercise is to determine who will benefit from your Mission.

Target Market Exercise

Whom will you serve? Your business must deliver products, services and/or information to someone interested in paying for those things. Who is that? Use these questions to come up with a profile of your Target Market.

- Male or female, or does it matter?
- Where do they live?
- What things do they buy?
- How much money do they make?
- What are their families like?
- What are their homes like?

The Name Game

Mission, Vision, Market and other terms that you find here have been defined in different ways in dictionaries and business books. As you work through *The Bare Bones Biz Plan* and build your Plan Binder, I will do my best to define the terms I use as I use them. Other experts, books and resources may use these words differently or use other tools to help you through the *Setting Sight* process. There is more than one way to skin a cat! Jeffrey Abrahams, author of *The Mission Statement Book: 301 Corporate Mission Statements from America's Top Companies,* says, "...the term 'mission statement' includes a broad range of approaches and titles by a wide variety of companies. Some companies put their vision or values before their mission, if they have one. Simply by shaping a 'statement,' these companies are stating or implying their corporate mission."

- What challenges do they face?
- What do they do for work?
- What do they do for fun?
- What do they value?
- Do they care about your Mission?
- What difference does your Mission make to them?
- How many people like this are there?
- What needs or wants do they have in common?
- What links them?
- Where are they?
- Where do they shop?
- Are there other businesses or organizations that could help you reach these people?

Spend time answering these questions. Then distill these answers into a brief description of your Target Market.

Tip You might want to name your Target Market or Target Markets. Consider a customer who has become a "raving fan" of your company. Adopt that name to refer to your Target Market, and to help you identify potential new customers.

Target Market Examples

At Bare Bones Biz, my Target Market *is…*

The small office, home office (SOHO) business owner who…

- employs 25 or fewer employees
- is internet savvy
- is in need of basic business tools, products and systems
- other businesses that also serve that business owner.

The Wackenhut Corporation provides security services. Wackenhut's Target Market *is government, industrial and business organizations worldwide. Simple.*

Washington Gas is a utility company in the District of Columbia. Washington Gas' Target Market *is the more than 700,000 residential and small commercial customers in the Washington, D.C., metropolitan and surrounding areas. Specific!*

Write down the description of your Target Market on the form called *Setting Sight* – Mission, Target Market. Put it in your Plan Binder.

You may want to keep the pages of notes that contain the more detailed descriptions of your Mission and your Target Market. As you work through these exercises, you can add to your Plan Binder. *The Bare Bones Biz Plan* will provide structure and discipline to your business-planning efforts. And it's flexible. Add pages as you want and need them. Just three-hole punch them and put them in the appropriate section.

This plan will repeatedly encourage you to reduce and distill your thoughts to the Bare Bones Basics. The clearer you are in your thinking, the simpler your plan, the more likely you will be to succeed.

> ► **TIP** You might want to name your Target Market or Target Markets. Consider a customer who has become a "raving fan" of your company. Adopt that name to refer to your Target Market, and to help you identify potential new customers.

Mission Statement, Target Market

Updated ____________

Your Mission Statement is WHY you are in business. What's the point?

YOUR COMPANY'S MISSION STATEMENT:

Your Target Market is made up of the people you intend to serve.

YOUR COMPANY'S TARGET MARKET:

Day THREE

Wednesday's Coaching Lesson: Focusing Your Vision And Discovering Your Unique Selling Proposition (USP)

Today, you'll create your Vision Statement. How will you know that you have made it in your business? What is the ultimate goal? That's your Vision.

"Plan or be planned for."
~Jim Abrams

Business expert Michael Gerber offers another way to express this. He asks, "What does your business look like when it's done?"

Like the Perfect Life, Mission Statement and Target Market exercises, the Vision Statement exercise is designed to make you THINK about your life and your business This is your most important work. Determine WHY you are in business, WHOM you will serve and WHAT you intend to accomplish. These pages in your business plan will guide you and help you make good decisions. Your Vision is the point on the horizon toward which you are sailing.

Now, let's craft your Vision Statement. How will you know when you have made it? What will it look like when it's done?

Here's a story to inspire you…

Ernest Shackleton was an adventurer. The early 1900s was a time of fantastic discovery and accomplishment: Everest, the North and South Poles… Shackleton set his sights on another first: A transcontinental trek across Antarctica, passing over the South Pole en route.

The *Endurance* set sail from England in August of 1914 and reached South Georgia Island, just off Cape Horn, South America. **The Vision, the ultimate Goal: Be the first men to cross the continent of Antarctica.**

"If you don't know where you are going, you'll end up somewhere else."
~ Yogi Berra

Leaving the island behind, Shackleton and his crew of 27 men set off for Antarctica, not imagining that it would be nearly 18 months before they would again set foot on land.

Shackleton's plan was sound. But weather rarely heeds a sound plan. That winter, the weather was particularly harsh. On January 19, 1915, with land only one day's sail away, the ship became locked in the ice. One crewmember described the ship in his journal as being "frozen, like

▶ **TIP** The problem with thinking is that it doesn't look like you are doing anything. In our action focused world, that can be a hurdle you are well served to overcome. Of the two, thinking trumps action. Clear thought leads to inspired, purposeful action.

an almond in the middle of a chocolate bar." The swirl of the Weddell Sea spun the ice and the imprisoned ship clockwise and farther from land. On October 15, 1915, the sturdy Endurance was crushed by the ice and disappeared into the sea below.

Consider Shackleton's dilemma. He and his crew were floating in the middle of the sea on chunks of ice. That night, Shackleton wrote in his journal, "I pray God I can manage to get the whole party safe to civilization."

Shackleton Crafted a New Vision: **The Whole Party Safe to Civilization.**

Notice the words he used in his journal. He didn't whine or bemoan the fact that the situation took a dramatic turn for the worse. He took full responsibility for the entire crew.

The men floated for *six months.* Imagine the constant darkness, the hunger, and, underfoot, the shifting, creaking, breaking ice floes. They slogged about, ankle-deep in slushy ice during the day. At night, ragged reindeer hides served as their sleeping bags. They ate all their provisions, and then they survived on seal meat and the flesh of their beloved sled dogs. Sea leopards saw the men as food and stalked them from underneath the translucent ice.

All the while, Shackleton served well as their leader and never abandoned his Vision. Shackleton did get every man to civilization. The rescue boat arrived on August 30, 1916, *two years* after *The Endurance* left England. That anyone survived is a miracle. Yet all 28 of them returned to civilization.

Vision Statement Exercise

What's your Vision for your company? What is your ultimate Goal? The "senior" goal? How will you know when your business is done? What will it look like? Spend some time thinking and writing.

Vision Statement Examples

- Microsoft's Vision is: A computer on every desk and in every home.
- Wendy's, the fast food chain, has this Vision: To be the customer's restaurant of choice and the employer of choice.
- Hotel business Marriott International has this Vision: To be the world's leading provider of hospitality services.

Distill your Vision into a concise statement and record it on the form called *Setting Sight* – Vision, USP, Elevator Speeches (see page 29).

Now, let's discover your Unique Selling Proposition (USP) and explore a succinct way to communicate that to the world… in particular, your Target Market.

► **TIP** Consider the market leaders in any industry. Very rarely are they the "low cost" providers. Avoid the "low cost" USP. Be willing to charge what you must to make good on an extraordinary USP.

USP and Elevator Speech Exercise

The first part of this exercise is to answer this question, what makes your company different and better than others that aim to satisfy the same customer needs or deliver a similar product or service? This is called your Unique Selling Proposition, your USP. You may complete this exercise alone or with help from your employees.

Note that unless you are WalMart, avoid settling on a USP that identifies you as the low-cost provider. That is a brutal USP, because you lose your advantage every time a competing company lowers its price. Instead, focus on what makes you smarter, faster, kinder, cleaner, better-smelling, more convenient, less confusing, easier to work with, more committed, more fun, uniquely qualified to serve your customers.

As with all of the *Setting Sight* exercises, this one requires high-level thinking. This exercise is difficult. It is so much easier to coast through life without asking big questions like this. You may not want to discover that your business is rudderless and unfocused.

Relax. You can do this. What makes you different and better? Write your answer on the form called *Setting Sight* – Vision, USP, Elevator Speeches (see page 27).

Next, work the USP into a short, attention-getting statement. It's called an Elevator Speech.

The Elevator Speech

Real Estate Sales Trainer Bernard Zick taught me how to create an Elevator Speech. The term "Elevator Speech" is inspired by the time spent with a stranger in an elevator. During the time it takes to get from one floor to the next, what could you say that would cause a person to perceive a need…and understand that you are the one to solve it?

Bernie's Elevator Speech format goes like this:

- "You know how…?" Hit them with their problem/challenge/heart's desire.
- "What we do is…" Fix it. Tell them what you do to solve that problem/help overcome that challenge/deliver their heart's desire. Include your USP.

Be creative! This format is flexible and designed to help you get started on your Elevator Speech. You'll know you have a winning Elevator Speech when the response is, "That's interesting! Tell me more."

Elevator Speech Examples

Dentists Howard and Mary Beth Shayne use this Elevator Speech:

> *"You know how a visit to the dentist can be a stressful event? At Foxgrape Dentistry, we specialize in pain-free smile brightening."*

Benjamin Franklin Plumbing promises customers on-time service and gives money back if the plumber shows up late. Here's the Elevator Speech:

> *"Have you ever waited around for a service company to show up? Frustrating, isn't it? I work for Benjamin Franklin, the Punctual Plumber. If there's a delay, it's you we pay."*

A woman at a local business association meeting greeted me with:

> *"Hi, I'm Kay of Kay's Landscaping. I'll care for your yard as if it were my own. And mine is beautiful."*

Elevator Speeches are useful! It's great to have a snappy reply to the standard question, "So what do you do?"

Sample Document Vision, USP, Elevator Speeches

Updated: ____________________

Your Vision is your senior Goal. As author Michael Gerber says, "What does it look like when your company is done?"

YOUR COMPANY'S VISION STATEMENT:

What is your Unique Selling Proposition (USP)? What makes you different and better?

YOUR COMPANY'S USP:

Your Elevator Speech is a brief response to the question, "What do you do?", highlighting your company's USP.

YOUR COMPANY'S ELEVATOR SPEECH:

Day FOUR

Thursday's Coaching Lession: Defining Your Values and Setting Your Goals

"Any time you sincerely want to make a change, the first thing you must do is raise your standards. When people ask me what really changed my life eight years ago, I tell them that absolutely the most important thing was changing what I demanded of myself. I wrote down all the things I would no longer accept in my life, all the things I would no longer tolerate, and all the things that I aspired to becoming."
~Tony Robbins

Today's first assignment is for you to create a list of Values. Values are "senior" policies that override all others, which you will always do (or never do).

Values Exercise

Start by creating a personal list of your core Values. It may be helpful to categorize them into the different areas of your life: spiritual, physical, family, community. An example of a spiritual Value is "I meditate daily," or "I attend church every Sunday." An example of a physical Value is "I eat an apple a day." Keep this list of Values short and focused on the few things that, if always done or never done, will positively impact your life.

Next, assemble a list of core Values for your company. If you are just starting your business, ask a trusted friend or prospective employee to help you with this exercise. If your business is up and running, you would be well served to have your team help you with this exercise. Most people wake up each day with the intention of doing the right thing. Spend some time with your employees discussing the behaviors that you will hold as your Values, your standards of performance. Ask and answer the question, "What will we always do (or never do) as a company?" This is a powerful, uplifting exercise.

Examples of Company Values

Here are a few of our Values at Bare Bones Biz, Inc.:

- We have fun at work.
- We demonstrate our integrity in everything we do.
- We operate from a written and known plan.
- We promote and develop leadership, freedom, respect, love, peace, creativity, accountability, humor, opportunity and prosperity.
- At Anheuser-Busch, their list of Values includes:
- Teamwork and open, honest communication
- Creating a safe, productive and rewarding work environment

- Promoting the responsible consumption of our products
- Preserving and protecting the environment and supporting communities where we do business

Note how these Values can impact decision-making for these companies' owners and employees. As you work through *The Bare Bones Biz Plan*, you will learn how to write Procedures for each aspect of the business. However, you can't foresee every possible situation that you or your employees may encounter. Your company Values will provide guidance in those situations that just aren't in the book. For instance, although its Values list is not so detailed as to explicitly exclude sponsorship of a beer-chugging contest at the University of St. Louis, it is absolutely implied by the third – and possibly the fourth! – Value on the list.

Use the form called *Setting Sight – Values* (on the next page) and write down your list of Values for your company. Check to ensure that the company Values complement and support your personal Values. Put the form in your Plan Binder in the *Setting Sight* section.

► **TIP** I don't buy the expression "It's not personal; it's just business." Your life is an integration of your personal, spiritual, physical, professional and financial values. Integrity is developed by acting in accordance with your core values in all areas of your life.

Sample Document Setting Sight – Values

Updated____________________

Your Values are your most important policies…what you will always do or never do.

YOUR PERSONAL VALUES:YOUR COMPANY'S VALUES:

Goal-Setting Exercise

Next up: Goals. Goals are "to have" statements. Goals are what you want to have from your company. Goals are measurable and achievable. Goals should be written down with a date attached to them. Goals are the milestones in the pursuit of your Mission and your Vision.

Look over your Plan Binder. Review your Mission and your Vision. Now set a timer for 20 minutes and start writing! Write down any ideas, to do's and projects that will move you closer to your Mission and your Vision. Don't judge, just write. If you get stuck, say a prayer asking for help and keep going. Aim for at least 101 ideas.

When the 20 minutes are up, go through the list. Identify 20 items that will have the most impact on achieving your Vision and fulfilling your Mission.

Craft those items into Goal statements:

To have______________________________

by _______________.

This list must include growth and profitability Goals. Don't buy into the myth, do what you love and the money will follow. That is not so. Confront your money hang-ups. Money is not at odds with living life at the highest spiritual level. Money is just a medium for exchanging energy. Understand that money is the lifeblood of your business. Without it, you'll be out of business and lose a wonderful way to be of service.

Put your Goals to the test. Are they achievable and measurable? Have you committed to the due date? Use numbers, dollars, percentages and hours to clarify your Goals.

Examples of Goals

Poor examples...Thumbs down.

- To have more money. (Not specific enough. How much?)
- To help mankind. (By doing what? By when?)
- To have more time with my family. (How much time?)

Good examples...Thumbs up!

- To earn net profits of 15% in 2012.
- To contribute 10% of profits to Habitat for Humanity every month.

101 Goals

Mark Victor Hansen, coauthor of the Chicken Soup for the Soul book series, encouraged me to write down 101 goals. He taught me that some goals will come to fruition quickly, just by writing them down. Once a goal is achieved, it ceases to motivate you. So a long list makes sure you have lots of great things to create and manifest.

- To spend no more than three weeks per month, 40 hours per week, actively involved in the business. This schedule starts January 2012.

Find the form called *Setting Sight* – Goals on the next page. You'll notice that this form references the Top Projects list. We'll introduce that list in the *Getting it Done* section of *The Bare Bones Biz Plan*. For today, just write down your Goals and organize them according to priority. Determine which Goals you will accomplish this year (short term) and which you will accomplish in the next 2 to 5 years.

You will have ideas, to do's and projects left over… items that you do not intend to act on right now. Write them down in your Master To-Do List. You can store them there, safe and sound. As you accomplish the Goals on your Goals list, you will replace them with new Goals. You can look through your Master To-Do List for the next ideas you intend to energize.

Do you struggle with Goal-setting? Are you afraid that you will list a Goal and then fail to make it happen? Are you afraid of failure? As author Susan Jeffries says, "Feel the fear and do it anyway."

Here's the good news: There are no Goal police who come and take you away if you don't reach your Goals. And you'll learn basic systems for accomplishing your Goals as you work through *The Bare Bones Biz Plan*, particularly in the *Getting it Done* section. Again, you can't do anything wrong here! List your Goals and we will work together to accomplish them.

Written Goals are powerful. Commit your Goals to writing and notice the whole universe conspiring to make them come true. Albert Einstein said, "The most important decision we will ever make is whether we believe in a friendly universe or a hostile universe." Why not decide friendly? The universe will support you.

Put the Goals page in your Plan Binder in the *Setting Sight* section.

Make goal setting fun and easy

If you don't hit your goal, the "Goal Police" don't come and take your children. There are no horrible consequences. You get to play again...tomorrow, next week or next year. Lighten up and keep Goal Setting in a positive perspective.

Sample Document Goals

Updated ____________

LIST AND PRIORITIZE THIS YEAR'S GOALS. GOALS WITH "A" PRIORITY SHOULD BE REFLECTED ON THE TOP PROJECT LIST. (SEE TOP PROJECT LIST IN GETTING IT DONE.)

A 1 ____

A 2 ____

A 3 ____

A 4 ____

A 5 ____

A 6 ____

A 7 ____

A 8 ____

A 9____

A 10 ____

B ____

B ____

B ____

B ____

BEYOND THIS YEAR'S GOALS – 2 TO 5 YEARS

Day FIVE

Friday's Coaching Lesson: The Executive Summary

"You'll never get it wrong and you'll never get it done."
~Esther Hicks, speaking for Abraham

Business is pretty simple. You are capable of learning what you need to know about business. And you are capable of doing it.

This week you have spent time THINKING and writing about what you want to be, to do and to have. Well done! Don't worry about doing these exercises right. You can't do them wrong! Just do them. As you progress through The Bare Bones Biz Plan, you will have opportunities to review, revise and redo your *Setting Sight* pages. You will continue to ask and answer the basic questions on these forms. The exercises in the *Setting Sight* section of The Bare Bones Biz Plan can be challenging. Let that inspire you! You are creating a wonderful business built on sound, basic business fundamentals. Congratulations!

Executive Summary Exercise

Today's assignment is to wrap up the *Setting Sight* assignments in a one-page summary of your business. This is called the Executive Summary.

On one page, answer these vital questions:

- What do you do? (Elevator Speech)
- Why? (Mission)
- For whom? (Target Market)
- What are your Goals? (Vision, Goals)
- How do you make money? (You'll update this section after Week Three - Making Money)
- Who else does this? (Describe your competition)
- What makes you better? (USP)

The Executive Summary is a standard component of all business plans. The format is flexible. The work you have done throughout this week has prepared you for this exercise. Review the previous exercises. Read through the pages in the *Setting Sight* section of your Plan Binder. Find and correct any inconsistencies. Can you see how your business is beginning to take shape?

Let's suppose you are an admirer of Warren Buffet, one of the world's smartest and most successful businesspeople. Imagine that you meet him at a seminar, a cocktail party or…in an elevator. You introduce yourself with your Elevator Speech. And Warren says, "That's interesting. Tell me more."

That's where the Executive Summary comes in. Your Elevator Speech is the 25-second summary of your business. Your Executive Summary is the 2-minute version.

In response to Warren's request to "tell me more," you could share your Executive Summary. Recite the main points and hand him a written copy.

Find the form called *Setting Sight* – Executive Summary on the next page. Craft a summary of your business, and keep it to one page. Longer than that, and you are wasting words. Brevity is clarity. Write your Executive Summary and add it to your Plan Binder in the *Setting Sight* section.

Remember, you will review and refine these pages as you work through The Bare Bones Biz Plan. Your business plan and your business are viable, growing, evolving entities.

As motivational speaker, trainer and author Mark Victor Hansen says, "Put your best work out there. Then, stand on its shoulders and make it better."

Putting it All Together

Let's go back to meeting Warren Buffet. Imagine that Warren is impressed with your Executive Summary and offers to meet with you for an hour in his office to go over your business plan. You accept his offer.

You bring your Bare Bones Biz Plan Binder to the meeting. You flip through it, section by section. This is your Bare Bones Business Plan.

Warren offers to…

- Buy your company for multiples of millions of dollars.
- Be on your board of advisors.
- Introduce you to just the right person who can help you reach one of your Goals.
- Whatever you imagine! Fill in the blank: _______________.

See how it fits together? This week you created the *Setting Sight* section of the plan. This is the foundation of your business. Well done! Next week, you will assemble the section for *Building the Team*. After that, Week Three is all about *Making Money*. And so on.

- Like any fitness program, there will be challenging moments. Press on!
- I promise you this: At the end of six weeks, your business and your life will be in much better shape.
- Open the Plan Binder and Share your Vision.

Share your Plan Binder with your team. Show them what you have been working on.

"Make no little plans, they have no magic to stir men's blood. Make big plans, aim high in hope and work and let your watchword be order and your beacon beauty."
~David Burnham

Practice your Elevator Speech on them. Let them know that you are committed to improving the company and to creating a place where they can grow, personally and professionally. Let them know that changes are coming. Change is stressful! However, it isn't right for you to play in the business game without a game plan. Let them know you intend to correct that. Let them know you are working a six-week Biz program that will help your get your company in top shape.

This announcement will scare some people. You know, there may be folks at your company who don't want you to look to closely at what's going on. Trust that this process is ultimately going to result in a stronger, more profitable and more ethical company. But there may be some painful moments along the way.

Your Weekend Homework

Spend a few minutes reflecting on this week's exercises. Jot down thoughts in your Journal. Building a business can be an amazing adventure. Capture your thoughts, feelings and moments of epiphany or frustration. Someday, you may reread these words or share them with someone else, and you will be well served by the wisdom you find in them.

Start using your *Master To-Do List.* Write down ideas, projects, to do's that need to be done and anything that needs follow-up. We will explore this and other tools for getting and staying organized in more detail in *Week Five – Getting it Done.* In the meantime, use the *Master To-Do List* as the one place you write down things that need to be done. No more writing notes to yourself on Post-its or little slips of paper.

Before you meet with a prospective investor or banker, ask them if they have a Biz Plan template they want you to use. If so, customize a new binder for them and pull into that template the appropriate sections of *The Bare Bones Biz Plan*. All Biz Plans have similar core elements.

Sample Document Executive Summary

Updated ___________________

This is a ONE-PAGE summary of your business…What you do, why, for whom, by whom, how do you make money, who else does this, and what makes you better?

▶ **TIP** Need More Direction? Remember, you can't do these exercises wrong. And you can always revisit these exercises and add to them. Give these pages your best effort. If you need help, enlist another business owner to be your Bare Bones Biz Buddy. Work through the exercises and build your Plan Binders together. Visit www.barebonesbiz.com. I offer Teleseminars on each section of *The Bare Bones Biz Plan*. Check it out! And you can always call or e-mail: 877.629.7647 and ellen@barebonesbiz.com. I am here to serve!

www.BareBonesBiz.com
877.629.7647

Day SIX

Monday's Coaching Lesson: The Clean-Up

"Success is a science; if you have the conditions, you get the result."
~ Oscar Wilde

Flip through the pages you created last week in the *Setting Sight* section of your Plan Binder. Do the words and pictures inspire you? Great! Now, let's take the next steps in *The Bare Bones Biz Plan*.

This week you will work through the *Building the Team* section of *The Bare Bones Biz Plan*. Today's lesson is simple yet super powerful. Today you are going to clean your desk.

Your desk says a lot about you. Is it a sane, functional, inspiring working environment? Or is it disaster on four legs? Certainly, a clean desk can improve your productivity. Even more importantly, cleaning your desk is a symbolic gesture. It symbolizes your willingness to change, to clear out habits and systems that no longer serve you. It symbolizes the business-building process. You are going to clean up each area of your business…day by day, step by step. Your desk is a significant part of the process.

And it shows your team that you are serious about building a better business. They will know you are committed when they see you pull your office apart, wash everything down and put it back together again.

A clean desk demonstrates to prospective employees that you are organized, professional and in command of your environment. People who value organization, professionalism and purposeful effort will want to work for you.

So far in *The Bare Bones Biz Plan*, you've been asked to think about and visualize what you want. Today, you are going to break out the elbow grease.

The Clean-Up Exercise

Start with your desk. Step by step, here's how to create a neat and functional working space.

- Collect the tools you'll need – a garbage can, a stapler, Post-it notes, paper clips, a marking pen and furniture polish or all-purpose cleaner.
- Take everything off your desk. Empty all drawers and shelves.

Set everything on the floor.

- Clean your desk, inside and out. Polish it, and make it shine!
- Go through every pile and get rid of stuff. Throw it out. You are no worse off having thrown it out if you can't find it anyway.
- Put everything you'd like to keep into "like kind" piles on the floor.
- Put back on your desk only the things you will need to access this week.
- Put back in your drawers only one of each type of office supply item you use.
- Put back on your shelves only current projects that require your immediate attention.
- Take the piles of like-kind information and file them.

A clean desk is no small thing. It is symbolic of your commitment to excellence, fundamental business basics and focused thinking. It is a testimony to your personal discipline. If you can't keep your own desk clear and your work focused and productive, then how can you lead others? A clean desk speaks volumes.

Look at the rest of your office. Business philosopher Lance Secretan says, "Your office is sacred space. It's where you work. Does it inspire you to create at the highest level?" Continue your clean-up efforts. If needed, paint the walls and mop the floor. Make your office representative of the lofty Mission and Vision you have crafted for your company.

Now, address the rest of the shop. Schedule a Clean-Up Day. Gather a few buckets and some cleaning supplies. Rent a power washer. Enlist your kids. Order a few pizzas. And clean your shop from top to bottom.

Cleaning is rejuvenating! Out with the old, in with the new! Whether you are just starting out or you have been in business for decades, make a clean start. Clean-Up Day... your clean desk...communicates that things are changing and they are changing for the better.

Professional Clean-Up Back-Up

Cleaning is easy...but not always simple. Are you a pack rat? Does the thought of throwing things away make your stomach hurt? You might need a Professional Organizer! Yes, there is such a person. Contact the National Association of Professional Organizers (NAPO) at 512.454.8626, and they can put you in touch with a local clean-up professional. Or check out www.1800gotjunk.com. These folks will show up and remove whatever you don't need anymore and sweep up afterward. They will even deliver appropriate items to the local recycling center.

Day SEVEN

Tuesday's Coaching Lesson: Creating an Organization Chart

"Some people are more talented than others. Some are more educationally challenged than others. But we all have the capacity to be great. Greatness comes with recognizing that your potential is limited only by how you choose."
~ Peter Koestenbaum

Today's lesson is about crafting the Organization Chart for your company. Tomorrow you will work on your company's Position Descriptions. These are useful tools for building your team.

Paradox: A statement, seemingly absurd or contradictory, that is in fact true.

What is a team? A team is something special that's created when individuals are free to do their jobs. Teamwork is a paradox. Team members perform individually, yet are dependent on the other members for their success.

Think of a college basketball team. The point guard is responsible for taking the ball down the court and setting up the offensive play. The center is responsible for controlling the area under the basket and scoring points from that area. The rookie on the bench is responsible for being ready, should the starting player get hurt or become unable to play. The coach's job is to bring out each individual's best performance to add to the overall success of the team. The Vision for each college team is to win the national championship.

Business, like basketball, is not a democracy. Someone has to be in charge. Someone has to lead. That's you. Your job is to develop and lead the team to realize the company's Vision and Mission.

How do you build a team? By helping individuals win. By helping each person on the team succeed individually and contribute to the whole. In his terrific book Good to Great, business author Jim Collins suggests, "Get the right people on the bus. Get the wrong people off the bus. Then, put the right people in the right seats."

An Organization Chart is a graphic representation of the main areas of your company, arranged according to reporting relationship. In other words, the Organization Chart lists who is responsible for what and who reports to whom. The Organization Chart represents the seats on the bus.

If you are migrating to business ownership from the corporate world, you may cringe at considering the formal structure of an Organization

Chart. Fear not! The Organization Chart can be a wonderful tool. Recalling my many, many jobs, I can count on three fingers the number of times I actually knew for what I was responsible and to whom I was required to report. I would have loved that information on every job. It's frustrating not to know what your responsibilities are. It's confusing to have someone tell you what to do, just to have another person tell you to do exactly the opposite.

▶ **TIP** Does the thought of an Organizaion Chart seem "too corporate" for your small business? If you want to grow, get over it. An "Org Chart" is a powerful tool for helping team members see how they fit and contribute to the whole.

Organization Chart Exercise

For this exercise, you will need...

- The page called Sample Organization Chart
- The pages called Sample Position Descriptions
- A large unadorned wall or dry-erase board
- A stack of Post-it notes...the 3-by-3-inch size is good.

Start by reviewing the basic company divisions on the See More Blinds Sample Organization Chart. The divisions are indicated by the double-lined boxes. Do the divisions reflect the main areas of activity in your company? Customize as needed. Note: You can use the Bare Bones Biz language for the divisions or substitute your own names.

What's not to love?

Identify Divisions and Responsibilities

Use Post-it notes to identify the divisions on your Organization Chart. Put them up on the dry-erase board.

On additional Post-its, list the Responsibilities for each division. Responsibilities are WHAT needs to be DONE to realize your Vision and Mission and achieve your Goals. Review the *Setting Sight* section of your Plan Binder.

Arrange the Post-its to show the reporting relationships. Who is dependent on whom? Who reports to whom? For example, note the Sample Organization Chart for the See More Blinds and Window Coverings company. Take a look at the Positions.

Don't be bound by what is currently happening in your company. Think more broadly. Think in terms of how the company should ideally operate. Plan for growth.

Create Positions and Assignments

Now group the Responsibilities into Positions for your company. Move the Post-its around until the Positions start to make sense to you. Name the Positions.

A Position Description lists the Responsibilities for that Position. Find the pages of Sample Position Descriptions for the See More Blinds and Window Coverings Company and use them as examples. A Position can be part time or full time.

Assign names to the Positions. Put the right people in the right seats.

Put your name at the top. You are the one responsible for *Setting Sight*. You are the leader. Understand that the Organization Chart flows uphill. If there is an empty Position, the person who holds the Position above it is responsible for handling that Position.

As you make your assignments, ask, "Can this person be successful in this Position?"

You may hold more than one Position. In a small company, each team member may hold a few Positions.

You may want to outsource one or more Positions. If you do, put that company's name in the box. On the Sample Organization Chart, notice that Mastery, Inc., handles mystery shopping services for See More Blinds, Inc.

As the company grows and as you hire more people, you can change the Position assignments. Add an additional box on the Organization Chart if more than one person is assigned to a Position.

Do your best to map out an Organization Chart that represents the basic divisions of your company and addresses the main Responsibilities of each division.

Draw your Organization Chart and write in names for the Positions. Insert a copy of your Organization Chart in the *Building the Team* section of your Bare Bones Biz Plan Binder.

One-Person Show or Ready to GROW?

Can you realize your Mission and Vision all by yourself? Does your Perfect Life describe your business as a one-person operation? It can be done. You'll still benefi t by creating an Organization Chart. All the areas oyour business need to be addressed. You will have to shift from Position to Position. The Organization Chart can make it easier to do that without get-ting confused. And you may decide to add a team member at some pointWhen you do, you can hand off one or more of your Positions.

Nothing stays static in the universe. Things are either shrinking or grow-ing. It is tough to make it all by your-self. As you work through The Bare Bones Biz Plan, open yourself up to the opportunity to grow and developa team. Maybe you have been burneby employees and you don't want to go through that again. A formal plan with written procedures and accountability systems will make teaming up a safer, saner experience.

If your Vision is of a big company, the Organization Chart can help you grow fast. Note on the Sample Orga-nization Chart that Suki is the Sales Manager as well as a salesperson. A small company doesn't need formal systems. By imposing the form of a larger company, you actually cause the company to grow. The systems drive growth. It works!

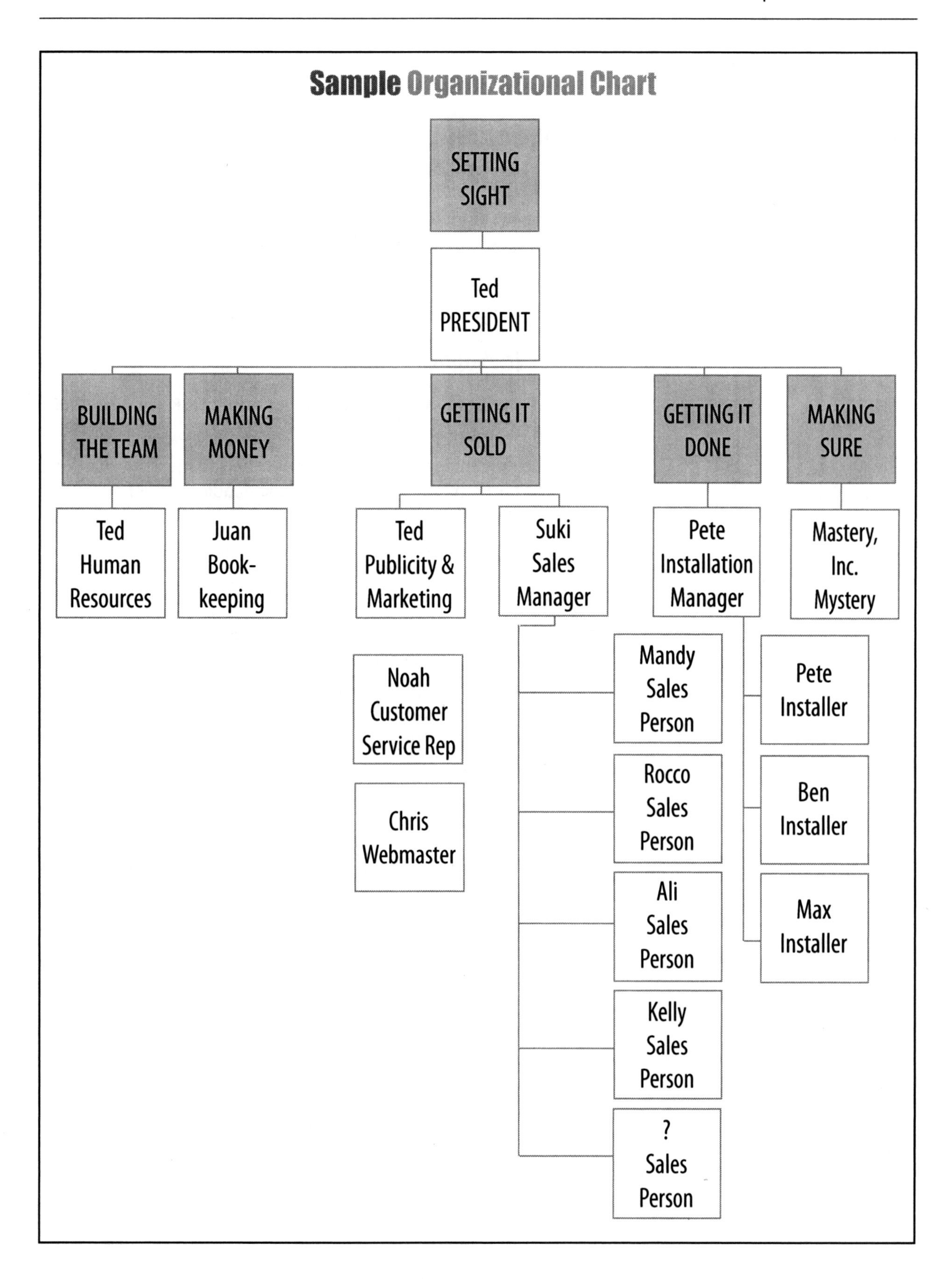
Sample Organizational Chart
SETTING SIGHT
Ted PRESIDENT
BUILDING THE TEAM
MAKING MONEY
GETTING IT SOLD
GETTING IT DONE
MAKING SURE
Ted Human Resources
Juan Book-keeping
Ted Publicity & Marketing
Suki Sales Manager
Pete Installation Manager
Mastery, Inc. Mystery
Noah Customer Service Rep
Chris Webmaster
Mandy Sales Person
Rocco Sales Person
Ali Sales Person
Kelly Sales Person
? Sales Person
Pete Installer
Ben Installer
Max Installer

Day EIGHT

Wednesday's Coaching Lesson: Who Does What? The Position Descriptions

"To do what you love and feel that it matters - what could be more fun?"
~ Katharine Graham

Today we will work on Position Descriptions. How nice it is to clearly communicate what needs to be done and who is responsible for doing it. Right-stuff people like the Organization Chart and Position Descriptions because they like being held accountable.

A Position Description is...

- A list of Responsibilities for the Position...basically, who does what.
- The percentages, dollars or key numbers to measure whether the Position-holder has successfully handled his or her Responsibilities.
- The compensation for that Position.

Don't worry about finishing every Position Description today. Just spend an hour on this task. If you have a team already, go over the Organization Chart assignments with each team member. Work with the person who holds the Position to flesh out that Position Description.

Position Description Exercise

Yesterday, you jotted down Responsibilities–things that need to get done–on Post-its and arranged them on the dry-erase board to help you create your Organization Chart. Refer to those Post-its as you list the Responsibilities for each Position Description. For examples, take a look at the Sample Position Descriptions.

Do the best you can to list the Responsibilities – what needs to be done – for each Position. As you go over the lists, ask and answer these questions:

- What needs to be done that we are not doing?
- What are we doing that doesn't need to be done?
- Who is served by doing this? The customer? The employees? The owner? The government?
- Does this help us make money, now or in the future?
- Is there a better, easier, faster or smarter way to do this?

► **TIP** Do they have the "Right Stuff?" Look for people who share your values. You can teach the "right" behaviors. I suggest you look for and recognize the core values before you hire.

- For the key numbers, come up with ways to measure performance in the Position. Ask and answer these questions:
- How can we measure performance in this Position?
- Is this a revenue-producing Position?
- What costs are associated with this Position?
- In this Position, how do I know when I have done a great job?

Ask every team member to think about his or her Position Description and to spend time editing or expanding the list of Responsibilities. For some, this assignment can be stressful. Perhaps Juan in bookkeeping is fearful that you may be preparing to replace him. He may interpret these questions as an indication of your distrust in him or displeasure with his performance.

Assure him that your intent is the overall improvement of every aspect of the company. Tell him about your Vision and your Mission. Let him know you would appreciate his help in building a better business–one that is of service to customers and provides a great life for the team members.

However, understand that he may choose to "get off the bus." It's all right. Consider your employees as volunteers. Every day, each one decides whether or not he or she is going to play the game with you. Some will love and support your efforts to improve the company. Others will not. The work you are doing to craft the Organization Chart and Position Descriptions will appeal to those who are inspired by your Vision and Mission. And it will serve you well as you recruit new team members.

For each Position, fill in the compensation section with what you are currently paying. Be aware that next week, in the *Making Money* section of *The Bare Bones Biz Plan*, you will put your Budget together. The Budget will help you determine how much you can pay for each Position. You may need to restructure your pay plan.

Again, this can be stressful. Communication is the key to keeping your team steady while you work out your business plan. Let them know that your intent is for your employees to make more money as you increase sales and productivity. For right now, just hold tight. Leave the pay as it is until we work through the Budget in the *Making Money* section.

As you complete the Position Descriptions, print a copy and store it in the appropriate section of the Plan Binder. For instance, the Bookkeeper Position Description goes into the *Making Money* section of the Plan Binder. You might want to store additional copies of all the Position Descriptions in the *Building the Team* section. For a downloadable, customizable Position Description Template, go to the Buy Stuff page at www.barebonesbiz.com.

RESPONSIBILITES ARE WHAT TO DO; PROCEDURES ARE HOW TO DO IT

Position Descriptions are incredibly powerful tools. Clearly communicating the Responsibilities for each team member is a loving, empowering gesture. Establishing ways to measure performance provides clarity and increased sanity to your company.

Responsibilities are what to do. Procedures are how to do it. For the Position Descriptions, just list the Responsibilities. You will learn how to write Procedures in the *Getting it Done* section of *The Bare Bones Biz Plan*. Over time, you and your team will create Procedures for each Responsibility.

As you go, you'll review your work and match it with your *Setting Sight* pages. Do the Position Descriptions fit in with your Vision and your Mission? Do they reflect your Values? Are you moving in the direction of your Goals?

Compare your Position Descriptions with your Organization Chart. Do you have the right people in the right Positions on the bus?

This is high-level work. I promised this would be an adventure. Congratulations on your progress so far!

"We must drop the idea that change comes slowly. It does ordinarily – in part because we think it does. Today changes must come fast and we must adjust our mental habits so that we can accept comfortably the idea of stopping one thing and beginning another overnight. We must discard the idea that past routine, past ways of doing things, are probably the best ways. On the contrary, we must assume that there is a better way to do almost everything."

~ Donald M. Nelson

Sample Document Position Description

Updated__________

Position: President See More Blinds and Window Coverings, Inc.

Name: Ted

RESPONSIBILITIES:

- Develop, empower and support the team in the realization of the Mission and Vision.
- Protect and grow the assets of the company.
- Complete The Bare Bones Biz Plan and communicate it throughout the company.

KEY NUMBERS:

- Goals as listed on the Goals form.

COMPENSATION:

- $60,000 per year

Sample Document Position Description

Updated____________________

Position: In Charge of Publicity and Marketing, See More Blinds and Window Coverings, Inc.

Name: Grace

RESPONSIBILITIES:

- Develop Marketing pieces.
- Update the Marketing Calendar twice a month.
- Determine marketing results.
- Develop the identity and branding package.
- Create and maintain a community service program.
- Communicate Marketing Calendar to the Sales Manager and the President weekly.
- Responsible for the Customer Service Representatives and Webmaster.
- Keep the customer service area clean.
- Deliver 20 Elevator Speeches weekly.

KEY NUMBERS:

- Number of calls received for our service and products at or above Budget
- Marketing and advertising costs at or below Budget
- Brand awareness survey

COMPENSATION:

- Base pay of $15 per hour
- 3% commission on all website sales

Sample Document Position Description

Updated____________________

Position: Making Money – In Charge of Bookkeeping, See More Blinds and Window Coverings, Inc.

Name: Juan

RESPONSIBILITIES:

- Daily data entry of sales and expenses
- Weekly Financial Quick Check report
- Weekly update of Year to Date Scorecards
- Month-end checklist and package
- Maintain detailed records of all Balance Sheet items.
- Maintain cash requirements.
- Payroll and subcontractor payments, bonuses and benefits
- Accounts receivable and accounts payable management
- Compliance with tax, payroll and insurance requirements
- Maintain excellent credit rating.
- Work with President and accountant to operate from a known financial position at all times.

KEY NUMBERS:

- Timely delivery of required reports
- On-time payment and compliance

COMPENSATION:

- $15 per hour

Day NINE

Thursday's Coaching Lesson: Attracting the Right People

"No matter how much work a man can do, no matter how engaging his personality may be, he will not advance far in business if he cannot work through others."
~ John Craig

Become a relentless recruiter. In fact, you should continue to recruit team members even after you hire them! Consider your employees a volunteer force. Every day they volunteer to come to work for you. The more compelling you are, the more compelling your Vision and Mission, the more people you'll find willing and even wanting to work with you.

Everything you have done so far in *The Bare Bones Biz Plan* will positively impact your company. You can see how you, your customers and your employees will benefit from your Vision.

If you are just starting your company, you'll find that *The Bare Bones Biz Plan* makes it easier to recruit, hire, train and retain great employees.

If you have employees already, they have been noticing the changes you've been working on the past few days. Some may be enthusiastic about the changes. And some may be terrified.

People don't like change. Remember the word homeostasis from your high school biology class? Homeostasis is the mechanism that controls body functions. It's what keeps your body temperature at 98.6 degrees as the air temperature around you fluctuates. It's what keeps you at about the same body weight, even if you change your diet. We are physically designed to avoid change. Change always produces some anxiety, and in some people, change can be downright frightening.

As you hit this point in *The Bare Bones Biz Plan*, employee turnover may throw you back into the fire. If someone leaves, the Responsibilities for his or her Positions fall back on you until you can find a replacement. You'll find yourself busier and crazier than ever.

You don't want to lose good employees. But you don't want to be held hostage, either. Stay true to your Vision and Mission. Recruit new and current team members by sharing what you see and why you are in business. Look for people who get it and want to help. And you are going to honor and reward those who want to play the game your way.

► **TIP** Creating a winning team is both art and science. Engage simple systems to recruit and hire. However, don't hire anyone you just don't feel good about. Life is too precious to spend with folks who make your stomach hurt.

Recruiting Exercise

Review your Organization Chart. What Positions might need to be filled now or in the near future? Find the form in the book called *Building the Team* – Recruiting Checklist. Customize a form for each Position you intend to fill. Put the page(s) in your Plan Binder under *Building the Team.* This will help you keep track of your recruiting efforts. A customizable version is available on the Buy Stuff Page at www.barebonesbiz.com.

Let it be known that you are looking. Get the word out. You are looking for great team members. Announce to your employees that you are going to need great people to help you expand. Alert them that you are not going to hire just anyone; you are going to be highly selective. And you know that they know fine people. Let them know that if they have a few people whom they would like you to meet, you'd be pleased to hear about them.

Remember Ernest Shackleton from last week's Vision Statement lesson? His initial Vision for his expedition was to be the first to cross the continent of Antarctica. He needed a team to accomplish the Vision, so he put this ad in a local newspaper:

> *WANTED: People to undertake hazardous journey. Small wages, bitter cold, long months of complete darkness; constant danger, safe return doubtful. Honor and recognition in case of success.*

Note that last line, "Honor and recognition in case of success". That compelling offer triggered hundreds of responses, including two from women.

You are growing your company with each new hire. Imagine patiently waiting and watching and selecting just the right people to help you take your company to the next level. Wouldn't it be nice to have the luxury of picking only the best for your company?

The right people are honest, willing and inspired by your Mission and Vision. Start looking. Expect to find them.

Don't Hire This Week!

Initiate your recruiting efforts. But wait to hire someone new until after you put together the Budget in the *Making Money* section of *The Bare Bones Biz Plan.* This will keep you from making a classic business mistake of putting the wrong person "on the bus." Today's lesson will help you expand your options so that you can make better choices when it's time to expand the team.

Use your Master To-Do List to jot down any to do's or follow-up actions that need to be taken.

Assemble your prospective team members and hold tight. When you are ready to hire, you'll make a better decision. And you may find people who are a good fit for your Board of Advisors. You'll learn more about that in tomorrow's lesson.

A Definition of Recruit:
Recruit comes from the French word recroistre, which means to grow up again. Webster defines recruit as to secure the services of, to seek to enroll.

Fly Your Flag!

Do you play well with others? Or are you a lone wolf? Are you the life of the party? Or would you prefer to skip the party altogether? Larry Bilotta is an expert on why people do what they do. He's created a terrific program called Flag Pages to help you and your team members discover your talents, strengths and motivations. Larry says, "Owners can use Flag Page technology to lead people in a way that builds loyalty by supporting their top motivations. Flag Pages can help employees control their negative emotions, grow their feelings of confidence and measure their inner progress so they can succeed at higher levels. And the Flag Pages system shows owners how to pick the people who will succeed in the company's culture and get along with the people already there." Your Flag Pages can help you find the right people and put them in the right Positions on the Organization Chart. Fly your flag! Contact Larry Bilotta for more information at www.flagpagetest.com.com.

Sample Document Recruiting Checklist

Updated ___________________

POSITION THAT NEEDS TO BE FILLED _______________________

SKILLS, TALENTS AND OTHER REQUIREMENTS FOR THIS POSITION:

WHO CAN HELP ME FIND THE RIGHT PERSON FOR THIS POSITION?

RECRUITING EFFORTS:

PROSPECTIVE TEAM MEMBERS FOR THIS POSITION:

Day TEN

Friday's Coaching Lesson: Shore Yourself Up With a Board of Advisors

"An executive is a man who decides. Sometimes he decides right, but always he decides."
~ John Henry Patterson

Imagine a helping hand and a friendly voice within reach at all times. Wouldn't it be nice if there were someone with whom to confer about the big decisions?

Today's lesson is how to create a Board of Advisors for your company. Advisors are unpaid volunteers with no real legal responsibility (as compared to a Board of Directors that comprises paid professionals who carry heavy legal and fiduciary responsibilities for your company.) Volunteers are naturally less formal in their advice and participation.

What does a Board of Advisors do? The best Boards are independent, objective thinkers who help you solve tough business problems. The best Board members complement you in strengths. They see your company with fresh eyes and unattached egos.

Board of Advisors Exercise

Start by putting together an ideal list of Advisors. Who are the best thinkers that you know of…living or dead? How about having Thomas Jefferson, Tom Peters, J.P. Morgan, Oprah Winfrey, Warren Buffet, Ben Franklin and Mahatma Ghandi on your Board? Cool, huh? Now, some of those folks are dead, and the others may be, well, over-committed at the moment. (But you never know. Ask them!) Add to your list others who exemplify the best characteristics of these great thinkers. Do you know someone with common sense like Ben Franklin? Warren Buffet would certainly add a high level of financial literacy to the Board. Who else do you know who really understands financial reports?

Pick folks who are smarter and richer than you. Don't be intimidated. Just ask. You want challenging people who will help you grow and develop. Aim for three or four crackerjack Board members. Pick the best people you can for the Board. Each member of the Board should feel honored to be in the company of such fine people. If someone turns you down, accept the rejection gracefully. Assume he or she is flattered that you asked.

Communicate what's required to be a Board member. What are you looking for? Direction or advice on a specific topic? You could ask for feedback about your Bare Bones Biz Plan. Meetings could be held monthly or quarterly. Go through your Plan Binder. You can certainly visit with Board members individually more frequently.

Help them right back. Just because they are smarter and richer than you doesn't mean that you can't be of service to them. Make sure that each Board member – particularly on a volunteer Board – knows that you are available to help him or her in any way that you can. Thank your advisors frequently for their efforts. Offer to help them right back.

Your Board can help you over the rough spots in business and can teach you important things...like how to become profitable. And how to manage more effectively so that you can have some fun in your life. But make no mistake about it, a company can't be run by a committee. You are ultimately responsible for the success or failure of your organization.

Add the names of your Board of Advisors to your Organization Chart. Store the page in your Plan Binder in the *Building the Team* section.

Your Weekend Homework

Write a personal note to every member of your team, including your Board of Advisors. Assure them that they are doing important work. Remind them of your Mission. Thank them for their help.

► **TIP** When recruiting a hard-to-reach prospective advisor, leave a compelling message with his or her assistant, or on voice mail. For example: "Hi Ms. Winfrey, I'm Ellen Rohr (877) 629-7647. I have a BIG idea for your Leadership School. And some good news about a local BIG GIVE project you've inspired. Reach me for an update...and thanks for all you do."

Week
Three:
Making
Money!

Day 11

Monday's Coaching Lesson: Getting to a Known Financial Position

"If he appreciates his lack of knowledge he will find a way to acquire it, and it is cheaper to learn before an investment is made in stock and fixtures, tools, etc., than it is to learn afterwards by sad experience."
~ Wesley Albert Fink –
Bookkeeping and Cost-Finding for the Plumber, published in 1918.

Today's lesson is about getting to a Known Financial Position (KFP). If you were driving 80 miles an hour in the dark with your lights off heading toward a cliff, would you like someone to yell, "STOP!"? OK.

Stop!

Do you produce financial reports – the balance sheet and Income Statement – every week? Do you analyze sales, costs, cash flow, and debt every week? If not, you may be heading for the cliff.

STOP. And find out.

A KFP is essential to your success and profitability. "Known" is the key element. It may be that you are losing money or deeper in debt than you would like to be. Find out how much and how deep. That's the starting place. The financial reports are the scorecards in the game of business. You can always improve the score, but you must know where you are right now.

This seems obvious. But from my experience as a business consultant, nine out of 10 business owners don't know where they stand financially. There are a couple of reasons for this:

- They don't know how to keep score.
- They are afraid to look, because they don't want to know how bad it is.
- If you are the one in 10 who runs, reviews and understands financial statements, congratulations!
- If not, well, that's going to change, starting today. Learning how to keep score is the focus of our lessons this week in the Making Money section of *The Bare Bones Biz Plan*.

Learning How to Keep Score

You'll be at a Known Financial Position when:

- You can generate Income Statement and balance sheet reports and trust that the information is current and accurate.

- You can go through the reports line by line, account by account, and understand what each dollar amount represents.

While often the most intimidating, the financial aspect of your business is the easiest one to get handled. Set your fear and frustration aside and have FUN keeping score.

I strongly recommend that you do your accounting "in house." You can't wait until the month is over to find out the score. You need to know the score while the game is on! The best way to do that is by generating financial reports in house. Your accountant may be able to train you on how to use your accounting software or recommend someone who can. You can also contact your accounting software company for a list of qualified trainers. Today's computers are so fast, and accounting software is so simple, you can do the accounting at your shop.

You are going to need some help, however, to get to a KFP.

- You need a good accountant. Many accountants just prepare tax returns. A good accountant will help you develop an accounting system that delivers the financial information you need to make good decisions. A good accountant will be excited when you tell him that you want to learn how to read and use financial reports. A good accountant won't feel threatened when you tell her you want to move the accounting system in house.
- A good bookkeeper is meticulous about data entry and getting it entered on time. In a small company, you may hold the Position of bookkeeper. This will serve you very well in the long run. Embrace the Position. Figure out double-entry accounting and how to fully utilize your accounting system. When you are ready to hand off the Position, you'll be prepared to work well with your bookkeeper to receive on-time, accurate and relevant information.

► **TIP** Don't be held back by an intimidating accountant, or one who acts like a martyr when you ask a question. Find a helpful professional interested in developing your financial understanding. Shop around!

Getting to a KFP Exercise

Schedule a meeting with your bookkeeper and accountant for sometime this week.

Go through the balance sheet and Income Statement, line by line, account by account. Ask these questions:

- Where do the dollar amounts come from?
- What do they represent? What do they mean?
- How does the information get entered into the accounting system?

Review how information moves through the company and ends up on the financial reports.

Keep it simple. Craft a chart of accounts that reflects your company. But don't overdo the detail. If you aren't going to use the data, do you have to track it? Do you need a separate account for electricity, trash removal, fuel oil and water service, or can you lump it into utilities.

Work together to answer these questions:

- How can we structure the chart of accounts to better reflect how we do business? How can we separate information so that we know how different divisions of the company are performing? Should we create divisions in the accounting system?
- Are we tracking information that we don't really need? At what cost?
- What will it take to generate current and accurate balance sheet and Income Statement reports at any time?

Finally, look over the Month-End Checklist together. Find the Month-End Checklist form in this book, or download the customizable form. Find it on the Buy Stuff page at www.barebonesbiz.com. This checklist makes sure that you stay in a KFP. Ideally, your bookkeeper completes the checklist. Your accountant can help by checking to make sure that your reports are accurate, and that all the legal and tax-compliance requirements are handled. Commit to completing the checklist every month, starting right now.

Don't delay. Insist on meeting this week. Insist on getting to a KFP by the end of this month. It is that important.

Store copies of your most current Balance Sheet, Income Statement and Month-End Checklist in your Plan Binder in the *Making Money* section. Write to do's and items that need follow-up in your Master To-Do List.

Good for you for your determination to acquire this knowledge!

Financial Reports 101

Don't know what a balance sheet is? Don't know your asset from your liability? Read *Where Did the Money Go? – Accounting Basics for the Business Owner Who Wants to Get Profitable*, by me. You'll learn the Bare-Bones Basics of the Balance Sheet, the Income Statement, the chart of accounts and double-entry accounting. You'll be delighted at how simple it really is! This information is the prerequisite for everything we discuss about accounting and finance in the Making Money section of *The Bare Bones Biz Plan*. Find this book on our Buy Stuff page at www.barebonesbiz.com, or call and order over the phone at 877.629.7647.

Sample Document Month-End Accounting Checklist

For the Month of: ____________________Year:__________

Actual Date:_________________________Prepared By:_________________________

Complete this checklist on or before the 10th of each month for the previous month.

Back up of the accounting system files.

- ☐ Run the Balance Sheet and Income Statement for the month…and go through line by line. What's different? What's "weird?"
- ☐ Review the General Ledger for the month and check for anything unusual or out of place.

Accounts Receivable/Invoicing

- ☐ Make sure that all sales for the fiscal period have been entered.
- ☐ If you job cost, make certain that all sales related to a specific job are coded to that job.
- ☐ Make sure that all payments and/or adjustments for the month have been entered.
- ☐ Follow up on any receivables that are more than 30 days overdue.
- ☐ Make certain that statements have been sent regularly.

Take a look…

- ☐ Print an aged Accounts Receivable report.
- ☐ The total of all Accounts Receivable should match the Accounts Receivable balance on the Balance Sheet.

Accounts Payable/Liabilities/Purchases

- ☐ Make sure that all vendor invoices, payments and adjustments for the fiscal period have been posted.
- ☐ If you job cost, make certain that all purchases related to a specific job are coded to that job.
- ☐ Post all purchases made by credit cards to their specific liability account.
- ☐ Make Loan Payments on Line of Credit Loans.

- ☐ Amount for Principal ______________

Take a look...

- ☐ Print an aged Accounts Payable report.
- ☐ The total of all Accounts Payable should match the Accounts Payable balance on the Balance Sheet.
- ☐ Print the detail for each credit card used for purchases.
- ☐ The outstanding balance of each card should match the corresponding liability account on the Balance Sheet.

Payroll

- ☐ Make certain that all paychecks for the period have been entered and posted to the correct expense accounts.
- ☐ Make certain that all payroll tax deposits have been made and posted to the correct expense and liability accounts.
- ☐ Make sure that the Payroll Clearing account has a ZERO balance.

Take a look...

- ☐ Double check that you have posted everything to the correct accounts – this is one of the EASIEST places to make mistakes.
- ☐ Review your payroll closely each month to avoid the costly mistake of fixing it later!

Banking

- ☐ Bank Accounts—make sure that you have reconciled all bank accounts according to the bank statement. Print the reconciliation report and staple it to the bank statement.
- ☐ Petty Cash—make sure that all payments that were made from petty cash have been entered, all deposits to petty cash have been recorded and the account has been reconciled.

Take a look...

- ☐ Bank Accounts—compare the reconciled balance to the bank's balance.
- ☐ Petty Cash—make certain that the total you actually have in petty cash matches the Petty Cash account balance on the Balance Sheet.

General Ledger

- ☐ Make sure Sales Tax is submitted
- ☐ Make sure all Insurance compliance issues are addressed.
- ☐ Make sure all tax reporting compliance issues are addressed.
- ☐ Make sure all new employees are properly accounted for in the accounting, information systems and with the Payroll Service
- ☐ Make sure that any journal entries for items such as depreciation have been posted.

Once all data entry is complete and all transactions that affect the fiscal period have been posted, you are ready to…

Create your Month-End closing package.

- ☐ Print the following reports:
  - ☐ Balance Sheet
  - ☐ Income Statement with Year-to-Date comparison
  - ☐ Income Statement with budget comparison
  - ☐ Most recent BBB Financial Quick Check report with the supporting financials
- ☐ Communicate any discrepancies, challenges, or anything out of the ordinary on the notes section of this checklist.
- ☐ Go with your intuition – if you think something looks "weird," or "off," or "wrong," make a note of it and report it to your Manager.
- ☐ If changes have been made to the BBB Basic Budget, make sure to update the budget in your accounting program and the Financial Quick Check.
- ☐ If you have difficulty balancing to any of the above accounts, use your detailed trial balance. Run the report for the account(s)in question for the specific period, and start looking. You might go back to a prior period and compare "then" to "now."
- ☐ Back up and store file off-site.
- ☐ Change the closing date in your accounting program.
- ☐ Write up any month-end notes.

If you're stuck, there's always help…call us at 877.629.7647or reach us online at www.barebonesbiz.com.

Day 12

Tuesday's Coaching Lesson: Bare Bones Budgeting Basics > Part One

Today and tomorrow, we will work on your budget. Budgeting is setting Goals for your company, for sales and for expenses, and then checking your Goals against actual results. Your budget is a powerful tool for creating your ideal business.

Spend at least an hour today in the budget process. The budgeting process is an ongoing activity. This week, you will jump-start your budget. Successful businesspeople know how to budget and use their budgets to make better decisions. Do your best and enjoy the process.

"Budgets are not merely affairs of arithmetic, but in a thousand ways go to the root of prosperity of individuals, the relations of classes and the strength of kingdoms."
~ William E. Gladstone

Getting started with basic budgeting

Start by stopping. Stop whining about budgeting. Stop claiming you can't do it. Stop claiming you don't get it. Budgeting is writing down what you intend to generate in sales and spend on expenses for a future period of time. You can do that. Over time and with practice, you will get better and better at budgeting. Any attempt at creating a budget is a positive move.

Realize your power. You are incredibly powerful, so much more so than you may realize. Writing your Goals, crafting your Budget… these actions trigger the realization of your Goals. Once you are clear on what you want, the whole universe conspires to help you. You have everything to gain and nothing to lose by budgeting.

Enlist a Budget Buddy. Working with someone is much better than tackling this process on your own. Two brains are better than one! Your Budget Buddy can help you come up with realistic Goals for sales and expenses and help you stay focused. A formal appointment to work on the budget may be just the discipline you need to get going on your budget. Who could be your Budget Buddy? Ask your accountant for help. Or seek out a member of your Board of Advisors. You can also work with one of your employees on the budget.

Gather your budgeting tools and financial information.

Pull together the items you need to begin making your budget. You can build a simple budget for any time period…a week, a month or a year. You can use Excel®, accounting software or paper to draft your budget.

- **Columnar pads are your friends.** You know those green-tinted sheets with the rows and columns inked in already? There is nothing wrong with using a pencil and paper to help you work out your budget.
- **Gather relevant information about the past two years' sales and expenses.** Print out your Income Statements for the past two years. If you don't have accurate Income Statements yet (yesterday you committed to getting to a KFP), your income tax returns will have some information about past years' sales and expenses. Also, your check register is a list of paid expenses. You can use that information to help you develop your expense Goals.
- **Compare apples to apples.** Make sure the list of accounts in the budgeting program matches the chart of accounts in your accounting program. Your accountant can help you do this. This will help you compare actual performance to budgeted Goals, item by item, account by account.

Basic Budgeting Steps

Start plugging in numbers for sales and expenses. The end result should be a "pretend" Income Statement that lists your Goals for sales and expenses for a future time period.

- **Enter the dollar amounts.** Work your way down the list of expenses. Reference your Income Statement, tax returns and check register to see how much you have spent on expenses in the past. Enter an amount that seems reasonable.
- **Fill in the sales line last.** Fill in all your projected costs, and then see how much you will need in sales to cover costs and leave your desired profit. Remember… the budget is pretend. You can move the numbers around.
- **Play the "what if" game.** Do several versions of your budget. Save each budget with a different file name so that you can reference each one. Creating monthly budgets allows you to better predict sales and profitability. Is your business typically busier in the holiday season? Reflect that in your budget. Are you considering a booth at a local trade show? Increase marketing costs in your budget for that month.
- **Think like a watermelon.** It only takes one seed to grow a watermelon plant. One plant can generate a dozen watermelons. Each watermelon is filled with hundreds of seeds. Theoretically, it only takes one seed to carry on the watermelon family. But Nature knows that "stuff happens" and plans for abundance. Do the same for your budget. Put a little cushion in the numbers.
- **The budget should show a profit!** Sales minus expenses should be a positive number. You may choose to create a short-term loss while you build your company. For instance, you may incur expenses before your company opens for

business. The best approach is to budget for profitability every month.

- **Keep a Budgeting Log.** You are going to pull some of your budgeted numbers from thin air. Write notes to yourself as you come up with the numbers for your budget. When you refer to your budget in the months to come, you may forget your assumptions. Write them down in your Budgeting Log.

Spend at least an hour today on budgeting. Store your work in the *Making Money* section of your Plan Binder. Tomorrow, we will continue working on your budget.

The budgeting process may make you aware of other projects and to do's that need to be addressed in your business. Keep your *Master To-Do List* handy...and jot those items down so that you won't forget about them.

More Help with Budgeting!

How Much Should I Charge? – Pricing Basics for Making Money Doing What You Love, by me, will take you step by step through the budgeting process. You learn how to use your budget to come up with a selling price. Find the book at www.barebonesbiz.com. We'll work together in real time to answer your budgeting questions.

Day 13

Wednesday's Coaching Lesson: Bare Bones Budgeting Basics > Part Two

"You don't get paid by the hour. You get paid for the value you bring to an hour."
~ Jim Rohn

Today you'll integrate your budgeting work with the *Setting Sight* and *Building the Team* sections of *The Bare Bones Biz Plan*. And you'll use your budget to create your pricing strategy.

Apollo 13 and Budgeting

Did you see the movie "Apollo 13"? Three astronauts take off for the moon. They put together a plan and laid out the space coordinates. Kaboom! Lift-off! And stuff happened. Pieces of the ship fell off, and the capsule ran low on oxygen. They circled the moon but realized they couldn't land on it, or they wouldn't make it back to earth. So they changed their plan. They knew what they wanted, ideally: Land on the moon, play some golf, take photos, hop in the spaceship and make it back to earth...alive. As the game progressed, they adjusted their Goal and decided that now the top priority was making it back to earth... alive.

So they headed home. And they had a plan for making it back to earth. They had the exact coordinates. They knew where they should be every inch of they way. And they were on course less than one percent of the time. They were too far to the left or right or north or south, or however one measures position in space. They adjusted and overcorrected and kept at it until they plunked down in the ocean on Planet Earth. Although the plan changed, without the plan, they might have missed the target altogether.

That's why you create a budget. Budgeting is an ongoing process. It's a cycle....Set Goals, play the game, keep score, make decisions based on the score, change you behaviors, revise your Goals, play the game again.

Check Your Budget Exercise

When you have put your budget together, give yourself a pat on the back. Now...let's check your work. Does your budget fit in with the rest of the work you have done building your Plan Binder and assembling your business plan?

Go through the *Setting Sight* section of your Plan Binder and check your budget against your Mission and Vision. Does the budget support your Mission and move you toward your Vision? Review your Values. Does your budget match up? Suppose one of your Values is to *provide a family-friendly work environment*. You may choose to include child-care services as an expense in your budget.

Look over your list of Goals. Is the sales line of the budget in agreement with what you wrote on your Goals list? If not, adjust one or the other...or both.

Review your Position Descriptions. Does your budget support the compensation you are offering your employees and yourself? In your budget, have you accounted for all the people who work with you?

Review and refine the forms in your Plan Binder. Make adjustments. The *Setting Sight* and *Building the Team* sections of your business plan should agree with your budget. Adjust the sales line on your budget to ensure that sales minus expenses delivers your Goal for profits.

▶ TIP

Once you've crafted a Budget, go back to the Executive Summary in the *Setting Sight* section. Refine the paragraph about how your extraordinary business makes money!

Check your budget to ensure that:

- Your budgeted sales Goal will support your intended expenses and your desired profits.
- The budget agrees with the rest of your business plan.

Now, let's use your budget to help you create your selling price.

Pricing Exercise

It's easy to make money. All you need to do is charge more than it costs. Sales minus expenses equals profits.

Simply put, the formula for creating your selling price is this: Divide your sales Goal by the number of widgets you can sell. That's your selling price per widget. For service work, divide your sales Goal by the number of hours, or days, you can sell. That's your selling price per hour, or per day, of service time.

Refer to your budget and crunch the numbers. *The Bare Bones Biz Budgeting Program* will automatically calculate your selling price per hour of service time. You can also play out different computations with pencil and paper.

Let's look at a simple example using See More Blinds, Inc. The budgeted monthly sales Goal is $120,000. On average, one month has 22 days of available work time...days available to sell, deliver and install window coverings.

$120,000 divided by 22 days divided by 2 installation crews = $2,727

Two installed sales per day, at an average sale of $2,727, will float the boat.

Note that this is just a simplified example! You need to crunch the numbers for YOUR business to come up with a reasonable selling price. *How Much Should I Charge? – Pricing*

Basics for Making Money Doing What You Love is a terrific book for explaining…in detail…how to create a budget and use it to support your selling price. If you haven't read it, do yourself a favor. Find it at www.barebonesbiz.com.

Also, note that this selling price for See More Blinds, Inc., will work IF the rest of the expenses and percentages fall in line. And IF the Salespeople are able to close enough calls to schedule two installations per day. As you move forward in time, you'll check your performance weekly. You can make adjustments to your budget, your pricing, your business plan, as needed.

Spend some time today working through several pricing strategies for your company.

You'll probably discover that your selling price needs to be higher… maybe a lot higher…than your competition. Remember, nine out of 10 business owners are driving toward the cliff. They don't know better because they don't look at their financial reports. They may be deeply in debt or going out of business. Calculate your selling price from your budget. Don't copy your competition!

To compete with lower prices competitors, you'll have to get creative.

Leverage Your USP.

Learn how to sell value instead of price. Become so much better than your competitors at what you do and how you do it that your clients will be happy to pay your prices. Your customers have gotten so used to poor service that it isn't even difficult to be extraordinary. Be polite. Show up clean and on time, and you will blow away most of your competitors.

What's your Unique Selling Proposition? How can you deliver it so well that your customers are delighted to pay more for your products and services?

Business is a lot more fun when you are willing to charge more than it costs.

Leverage Your Time with Products and Information.

If your business is limited to skilled services, you are going to have to charge enough money per hour to cover all expenses and make a profit. Your skills are valuable and your time is limited. Let your budget be your guide and price accordingly.

No matter how much you charge per hour, you still only have a limited number of hours per day per service provider. Think about ways to leverage your time…with products and information.

Jack Welch, former CEO of General Electric, is considered one of the greatest business leaders in history. If you want Jack to speak at your local chamber of commerce event, he would charge you about $50,000…if he had room for you on his schedule. If you wanted to visit with Jack personally to ask for his business advice, the price would be much higher. But you can buy Jack's book, *Jack – Straight from the Gut,* for about $24. Jack leveraged his time by selling his advice in book form. And he sold millions of books!

Is there a way to deliver what you do or know without offering your time? Consider writing what you know and selling that information in books, magazines or on the

Internet. Can you create a DVD or videotape that teaches others how to do the wonderful things that you do? Can you develop a product line that supports your services? For instance, See More Blinds, Inc., could sell "mini-blind duster mitts" along with installed window coverings.

Most business owners never put any thought into their pricing! Most of them call their competitors, assume a fake voice, ask how much they charge…then charge just about the same thing. Most small businesses fail! You can't win by blindly following the competition. Good for you for taking a fresh look at your pricing.

Summarize your pricing decisions on the Pricing form. If you have decided to add new products or services, make adjustments to your budget for sales and expenses. Put the form in the *Making Money* section of your Plan Binder. Reflect on your experiences and jot your thoughts down in your Journal.

This is the budgeting process: Set Goals, play the game, keep score, make decisions based on the score, change you behaviors, revise your Goals, play the game again. Tomorrow, we'll introduce a wonderful way to help you match budgeted Goals to actual performance on a weekly basis.

Next week, we will spend time in the *Getting it Sold* section of *The Bare Bones Biz Plan*. You'll lay out your plan for marketing and selling your wonderful products and services…at the right price.

Bootstrap

As you put together your budget, you may need some money to get your business started. The technical term is start-up capital. When you borrow this money from someone, or from a bank, it's called venture capital. You are best served by borrowing as little as possible to start your company. Even if you have a billion dollars, or access to a billion dollars, create a business plan that depends on sales income to cover expenses right out of the gate. It will discipline you to operate in a responsible, frugal manner. Pull yourself up by your bootstraps! Count on yourself and your business to grow through the sale of your goods and services.

Pricing Strategy

See More Blinds and Window Coverings, Inc. Updated

BUDGETED SALES GOAL PRICING STRATEGY THAT WILL HELP YOU REACH YOUR GOAL

- $120,000 per month divided by 22 work days per month = $5,455
- Each two-person installation team can do one See More Home Renewal installation per day.
- Our selling price for the See More Home Renewal package will be $2,727
- HOW DOES THIS COMPARE TO YOUR COMPETITORS' PRICING STRATEGIES?
- In-A-Blind, Inc., offers a similar package for $1,999.
- However, In-A-Blind does not offer our lifetime warranty and cleaning service.

Day 14

Thursday's Coaching Lesson: The Financial Quick Check

Today you'll learn a simple way to take the pulse of your company by reviewing a one-page report: The Financial Quick Check. This powerful report is a weekly summary of the few numbers that make all the difference to the success of your business.

"When we change the models in our mind, we change the results in our life."
~Mark Victor Hansen

Financial Statements – The "Reader's Digest" Version

When I first learned how to read and use financial reports, I would assemble the information to show my partner and husband, Hot Rod, how we were doing. I'd cover his desk with pages and pages of financial reports. His eyes would glaze over.

One day he sighed and said, "I really hate this. I'm glad you know what this means, but I can't take all this information. Can you just show me the few numbers that make all the difference in our company? Can you give me the 'Reader's Digest'version?" Hmmmm. Hot Rod was onto something.

▶ **TIP** Notice a group of grade school kids playing a game at the park. They will keep score. It's more fun when you do. The Financial Quick Check is the Company Scorecard. There is always something you can do to improve the score.

When it comes right down to it, there are only a few numbers that make all the difference. If there is a problem with one of the critical numbers, you can dig deeper and get more information. If you were to watch the critical numbers at your company, you would have a pretty good idea of what is going on. You would know for certain whether or not you are *making money*. You would know if you are going to have enough money to cover payroll.

Gail Gudell is a professional organizer and bookkeeper, par excellence! She is also my sister and in charge of *Making Money* at Bare Bones Biz. Gail started working with us many years ago and is one of the reasons Hot Rod and I didn't kill each other in our early years of working together. Gail and I sat down, determined to put the few numbers that make all the difference on a single sheet of paper. This is what we came up with. (Thanks, Gail!)

Financial Quick Check Exercise

This simple, powerful form summarizes the most important financial information from the Balance Sheet and Income Statement. Take a look at the Financial Quick Check form. You can print and use this form as is, or download a customizable version at www.barebonesbiz.com. It's included in The Complete Suite on the Buy Stuff page.

Understand that you have to be at a KFP to successfully use the *Financial Quick Check.*

If your accounting program allows you to assemble a neat, consolidated report like this, that's cool. However, we still recommend that you or your bookkeeper manually enter your financial information into the Financial Quick Check Form. That "manual moment" causes you to confront the data. It will help you stay at a KFP. You'll be able to find and fix mistakes so much easier when you are checking the financial information on a weekly basis. And the Quick Check will help you break out of denial if denial is keeping you from charging the proper selling price.

I recommend filling out this form every week. Have it on your desk by noon on Monday for the previous week.

To complete the form, print your current Balance Sheet and Income Statement reports. Summarize the critical numbers from those reports on the Financial Quick Check form.

Time Period

This form is set up to compare a period of time – I recommend filling this form out weekly – to the Year To Date (YTD) totals. List the budgeted information for the same period of time. Now you can compare actual performance to budgeted Goals.

Note the percentage columns. Numbers vary from day to day and week to week. Percentages present a clearer picture of trends and performance. By tracking critical numbers as a percentage of sales, you can assess data from different time periods. This makes it easy to see if you are on track...or way off.

Ratios

The Cash Flow Ratio matches cash and accounts receivable against current accounts payable. If you have $20,000 in cash, $40,000 in accounts receivable and $30,000 in accounts payable, your Cash Flow Ratio is:

$$\frac{\$20{,}000 + \$40{,}000}{\$30{,}000} = \frac{\$60{,}000}{\$30{,}000} = 2 \text{ to } 1$$

In other words, for every dollar of bills you have to pay, you have two dollars in cash and accounts receivable with which to pay it. This is helpful data! Keep in mind that if your accounts receivable are more than 60 days old, you probably won't collect all of them. Recalculate this ratio using 30-days-or-younger accounts receivable to be conservative.

The beauty of knowing this ratio is that it will motivate you to collect your accounts receivable. Also, stop the work-now-bill-later madness! A collect-on-delivery sales policy will dramatically improve this ratio...and your cash position.

Use the Data to Make Decisions.

The financial information tells you the score. The numbers tell you what is happening, but not why it is happening. If a dollar amount or a percentage is off, investigate. It may be an accounting mistake. If not, look into what's happening to cause that score. Then figure out how to make it better.

Suppose sales are less than anticipated for this week. You could initiate a sales contest and offer performance awards to your sales team. You could call people on your customer list and offer a special product. And you could hold off on buying that new coffee pot until next week. Make sense? Take action to increase sales and maintain profitability with the sales you have right now. You can act quickly because you are operating from a KFP.

Remember to think like a watermelon. If your sales amount is too skinny, it's harder to make a profit. Get the top line where it needs to be. Certainly, you can look for ways to better manage expenses. Address the differences between budget and actual performance throughout the company. But understand that the top line – sales – has to be big enough to cover all the costs of doing business, including reasonable compensation and benefits for you and your employees. Get the top line to budgeted Goal level, and lots of problems go away.

Customize Forms for Your Company.

Feel free to customize this form to best suit your company. You might want to create a form like this for each division at your company. You could customize a form like this to keep track of a big project. You could add numbers for callbacks, customer complaints, compliments or safety violations. Keep it simple and real. Be consistent with your tracking.

Produce this report every week and you will sleep better every night. This is a vital part of your ongoing system for operating at a KFP.

Keep the most current copy of the Financial Quick Check in your Plan Binder under the *Making Money* section. You may choose to include a current Year to Date actual performance matched to Year to Date budget version of this form in your Plan Binder, too. The Financial Quick Check is an easy way for you to keep score...and stay at a KFP. When you show your Plan Binder to your Board of Advisors, your investors, or bankers, the Financial Quick Check makes it easy for them to see what's happening at your company.

Tomorrow, we will discuss Open Book Management and how to help your employees develop their financial literacy. You can use the Financial Quick Check form to teach your employees financial basics. Use it to show them why you need to charge what you charge. Too much financial information can be overwhelming; this form is just the right size.

Financial Quick Check

TIME PERIOD: ____________ PREPARED BY: ____________

	Month To Date		COMPARED TO Budget/Goal		COMPARED TO Year to Date	
SALES						
SALES - Service	$ -	____%	$ -	____%	$ -	____%
SALES - Construction	$ -	____%	$ -	____%	$ -	____%
SALES - Coupons & Discounts	$ -	____%	$ -	____%	$ -	____%
SALES - Customer Refunds	$ -	____%	$ -	____%	$ -	____%
SALES - Subcontractors - Other Trades	$ -	____%	$ -	____%	$ -	____%
SALES - Total	$ -	____%	$ -	____%	$ -	____%
DIRECT COSTS (COGS)						
COGS - Materials - Service	$ -	____%	$ -	____%	$ -	____%
COGS - Direct Labor - Service	$ -	____%	$ -	____%	$ -	____%
COGS - Materials - Construction	$ -	____%	$ -	____%	$ -	____%
COGS - Direct Labor - Construction	$ -	____%	$ -	____%	$ -	____%
COGS - Permits	$ -	____%	$ -	____%	$ -	____%
COGS - Equipment Rental	$ -	____%	$ -	____%	$ -	____%
COGS - Subcontractors - Our trades	$ -	____%	$ -	____%	$ -	____%
COGS - Cash Discounts Taken	$ -	____%	$ -	____%	$ -	____%
DIRECT COSTS (COGS) - Total	$ -	____%	$ -	____%	$ -	____%
GROSS PROFIT/GROSS MARGIN	$ -	____%	$ -	____%	$ -	____%
OPERATING EXPENSES (OVERHEAD)	$ -	____%	$ -	____%	$ -	____%
NET PROFIT	$ -	____%	$ -	____%	$ -	____%
TOTAL PAYROLL	$ -		$ -		0	
TOTAL PAYROLL AS A % OF SALES	____%		____%		____%	
CASH FLOW and QUICK RATIO						
Total Avaliable Cash from Checking & Savings	$ -					
Accounts Receivable	$ -					
Total (A)	$ -					
Accounts Payable (B)	$ -					
Cash Flow (A) - (B)	$ -					
Ratio (A) / (B)	____ to 1		____ to 1			

Toss It, File It or Keep It in Your Plan Binder?

Each week, you'll go through your Plan Binder and update it. Keep the most current copy of each of the forms, checklists, budgets and financial reports. When you update it, decide what to file and what to throw out. Pack rats, listen up! You can streamline your office and your life if you throw out stuff you won't look at again. For filing help, we heartily recommend a filing system called The Paper Tiger. GREAT tutorial on the keep-or-toss question…and a sure-fire system for finding anything you choose to keep in five seconds or less. I use this system at Bare Bones Biz, Inc., and I don't waste any time looking for things. Find The Paper Tiger at www.thepapertiger.com.

Day 15

Friday's Coaching Lesson: Open the Books — Bare Bones Business Literacy for All

"Life is a game. A game consists of freedom, barriers and purposes."
~ L. Ron Hubbard

To *open the books* means to share *real* financial data with your team. Today we'll teach you how to open the books and let your employees in on the game.

What's the big secret about financial reports? Why do businesspeople treat the financial reports as if they were CIA Top Secret Classified information? Why are we so sensitive about the data?

The answer is because the numbers tell the truth. Sure, you can wear a fancy suit and sit at the head table at your chamber of commerce dinner meeting. But the numbers will tell if you are really winning or losing the business game. You can say that your employees are your top priority, but the numbers will tell if you spend any money on them. The numbers and the dollars tell the score.

The Great Game of Business

It doesn't make sense to ask people to play a game with you and then withhold the score from them. Won't it make the game more fun if everyone knows the score?

Give your team a great game to play. This week you have raised your prices to support your Goals. Unless you share your financial reasons for raising your prices, your team might think you are just being greedy. Employees sometimes think that 100% of the difference between what they are paid and what you charge ends up in your pockets. This is a good time to open the books.

Open-Book Kick-Off Exercise

Schedule a meeting with your team to share your plan and sell them on your new prices. Bring your Plan Binder to the meeting.

Start with an overview of *The Bare Bones Biz Plan.* Let your team know that you are committed to creating a great company. Recite your Mission and Vision. Read through your list of Values. Flip through the Plan Binder and show them how you are building your business plan. Thank them for their help.

Show them what goes into the selling price. On a dry-erase board or flip chart, list all the expenses that need to be covered by your price. Show them what's in it for them... benefits, education, vacation, retirement, and salaries befitting employees of their caliber. Show them what is in the price for the customers' benefit... top-grade equipment, quality products and services, community contributions. Professional and ethical business practices require money. Show your employees your justification for the selling price, because if they don't buy your prices, neither will your customers.

Your employees may or may not be interested in the numbers. For those who are interested, offer to go into detail in one-on-one financial education sessions. For those who don't want more detail, your willingness to share the data is enough. It builds trust.

Be worth it. If you are going to be more expensive than your competitors, you are going to have to be a lot better than they are. Let your team know that's why you have been cleaning the place up. Show them what's in your budget for upgrading your vehicles and equipment, creating a formal training program, etc. Discuss how you can do more for your employees and your customers in every area of the company.Let them know that you value them...and feel good about charging a premium price for the products and services that they deliver.

Let them know you will hold them accountable, and teach them the skills to win. Your employees will better understand the need for good data if they see how you use the data to establish selling prices. You need to know if the numbers and dollars built into your prices are going to cut it in the real world. You need to keep score.

You also need to know how much they are selling (or not selling). Based on your budget, you need so much in sales each day, week, month, and year. Let them know that next week, you will be introducing Scorecards so that they can help you gather good data. They probably won't be super-excited about more paperwork. However, the information is essential. Without it, you are driving blind.

Keeping score will also help you help your employees. How are they doing in sales, productivity, call-backs, customer complaints? If you know the score, you can help them get better. Perhaps the best part of playing a great game is helping willing team members become winners.

As you wrap up this week, remember to jot down any to do's and projects on your Master To-Do List. And use your Journal to record any insights gained from your adventures this week.

Your Weekend Homework

At this point in *The Bare Bones Biz Plan,* you have confronted the numbers and dollars and, more than likely, significantly raised your prices. Congratulations! You and your team will make more money!

One of the best things about money is the joy of giving it away! Money is meant to flow, to energize and to enliven that which it touches.

Don't wait until you have plenty of money to start giving it away. That's backwards. Give, and you shall receive. Financial management guru Suze Orman puts it this way:

> *Beyond a shadow of a doubt, I now know the following principle is true: We experience prosperity, true financial freedom, when our actions with respect to money are dharmic, or righteous, actions – that is, actions of generosity, actions of offering.*
>
> *I knew I always felt better right after I made an offering – stronger, worthier, more powerful. And after a while I began to believe that it was no coincidence that after I made such an offering, more money would always begin to flow my way.*

Make giving a part of your corporate culture. This weekend, find a community project that warms your heart. Determine a dollar amount or a percentage of sales that you will commit to the project on a monthly basis. Build your contributions into your budget. Let everyone who works with you in on the power, the magic, the wonderful feeling that comes from giving to those in need.

Read The Great Game of Business

Get to know Jack Stack, the author of *The Great Game of Business* and the poster child for the Open Book Management (OBM) movement. Learn more about opening the books at www.greatgame.com.

Week
Four:
Getting
it Sold

Day 16

Monday's Coaching Lesson: Overcoming "Salesphobia"

"Keep your focus on sales. If the top line is right, managing your business is easy. If the top line is too low, everything is a struggle."
~ George Barnett

The Bare-Bones *most important part of business* is sales. Every area of your business, all of your planning, all of your systems, should support sales.

Does that make you uncomfortable?

> *Salesphobia:*
> *1. A compulsive and persistent dread of or aversion to sales.*
> *2.Any strong aversion or dislike of sales.*

Sales is the name of the game. "Salesphobia" is a fatal disease. If you or someone on your team suffers from salesphobia, it will absolutely kill your business. Luckily, the condition is curable. In today's lesson, you'll learn the causes of salesphobia. Then we'll start you on the road to recovery.

"My name is Ellen, and I am a recovering salesphobic."

Once upon a time, I exposed my salesphobia during a planning session with one of my clients. We were working together to develop a curriculum for the service managers' training program. One of the other committee members said, "The service manager has only one responsibility: sales. The service manager needs to look at every situation he encounters and ask, 'Is this helping or hindering sales?'"

Certainly, the technical aspects of the job were as important as sales. What about *making sure* the service trucks were in top shape? What about safety issues?

I argued, "Money isn't the only thing, you know. There's more to a business than making sales."

His head whipped around. He took a deep breath and replied, "Unless a sale happens, none of those other things will happen. Sales have to be the top priority. Ellen, what is your problem with sales? I'm not talking about selling people things they don't need. I am talking about solving problems and charging a reasonable price. You've got an issue with sales. And you need to get over it."

He was right. Sales is the game. That confrontation knocked some sense into me. Certainly, I am not the only one eligible for a 12-step program for recovering salesphobics. In his fabulous book How To Sell At Margins Higher Than Your Competitors, Lawrence L. Steinmetz makes this observation:

Many salespeople really don't like selling. In fact, a lot of salespeople think selling is just a notch above ambulance chasing. The truth is, more than 40 percent of the salespeople I've tested fundamentally don't approve of selling – and my educated guess is that about 90 percent of our total population doesn't approve of selling.

If salespeople don't approve of selling, and if 90% of all people don't approve of selling,...no wonder so many businesses fail!

Are You a Wimp About Sales?

You may dislike sales because you've had bad sales experiences. Have you ever been hounded by the car salesman who won't stop asking, "What will it take to earn your business today?" Have you ever been assaulted with a spray of cologne while walking through a department store?

As a result, you've learned to hate sales and cringe at the thought of being a salesperson. But there is a paradox here. The things you don't like about sales are things that don't work in sales. You don't like pushy salespeople. You know what? Pushy salespeople don't make many sales. You hate it when salespeople lie. Well, liars don't make a second sale, which shortens their careers in sales. Fears about sales are founded in behaviors that don't create sales!

And there's the fear of rejection. You don't want to ask someone to buy and have them say no. To be successful, you must transcend this fear. If you or a team member is a salesphobic, you better get on the road to recovery.

Overcoming Salesphobia Exercise

Today's exercise is to become aware of sabotaging, salesphobic thoughts and actions in your company. Review these points to increase your sales appreciation.

- **Recall purchases that made you happy.** Today, you've bought power, water, sewer, Internet service, phone service, fuel...without even thinking about it. Because it's so convenient, you agree to have these basic goods and services constantly delivered. Think about your ongoing purchases. Over time, with financing, you're buying your car and your house. During a month's time, you've bought food, clothes, entertainment, education, haircuts, vitamins, school yearbooks, family outings. Fun stuff! Wonderful purchases. Without sales, you would spend all day every day gathering food and water and obtaining basic clothing and shelter.

- **Realize the connection between sales and world peace.** Good sales are good trading practices. Good sales allow you to focus your energies on your skills and talents and offer them to the world in exchange for money. Then you can offer that money to others to secure their livelihoods while benefiting from their skills and talents. Good sales build solid communities and our best chance at world peace. Certainly, governmental distribution of goods and services is a poor substitute for free-market trade.

- **Understand that without sales, you are out of business.** It's easy to go out of business. It's easy to lose money in business. Either way, you do a disservice to yourself, your employees and your customers. As a profitable business owner, you are a pillar of society. As a losing business owner, you are a burden to society.
- **Promise never to sell anything your customers don't need or want.** Does that make you breathe easier? Good sales and good customer service go hand in hand. Offer customers your best, and ask them if they would like to buy. Good sales feel good to everyone involved. Sales expert Bill Stiles says, "Think of yourself as your customer's assistant buyer. Your customer has a problem. Offer solutions. Help solve the problem."
- **Accept that people want to buy from you!** Review your Unique Selling Proposition. Aren't your customers better off if they BUY?

Now, get out there and sell

Let people know about your great business. Today, and every day this week, you and each of your employees will…

- **Deliver 10 Elevator Speeches.** Find 10 people, preferably strangers, and deliver your Elevator Speech. Hand out your business card, too. Watch for their reactions. Do they react positively? Do they look bored or confused? Do they laugh? Review your USP and revamp your Elevator Speech until it causes people to respond with, "That sounds interesting. Tell me more." Ask them what business they are in. Listen. Share an authentic human moment.

This exercise will expose any salesphobia at your company. Discover the sales-lovers on your team. Uncover the salesphobics. You are going to help them overcome their fears. Or they are going to "get off the bus." Tomorrow we will lay out a Bare-Bones basic system for creating a sales-focused company.

The game is SALES. It is an honorable game. Good for you for playing!

You may want to update your Elevator Speeches in the *Setting Sight* section of your Plan Binder. Also, keep assembling ideas, to do's and projects on the Master To-Do List. We will work on organization and strategies for *Getting it Done* next week.

Day 17

TUESDAY'S COACHING LESSON: CREATING A SALES-FOCUSED COMPANY

"That which you recognize, you energize."
~ Mark Victor Hansen

Today, you'll learn about sales management, and you'll start assembling the *Getting it Sold* section of your Plan Binder.

Growing a sales-focused culture doesn't just happen. It requires the intention to deliver your Unique Selling Proposition. It requires paying attention to sales and *making sure* all systems support the flow of products and services to your customers. It takes sales management. A solid sales management program includes accountability for sales, sales training, and honor and recognition for sales success.

Salesperson Scorecards.

To play the game, you need to keep score. The Salesperson Scorecard imposes accountability for sales. Implementing this form will increase sales and performance at your company. Take a look at the sample Salesperson Scorecard in this book. You can download a customizable version of the Salesperson Scorecard at www.barebonesbiz.com on the Buy Stuff page. (Bare Bones Biz' Shauna created the Excel form. It keeps a running total of the Salesperson's performance all year. Thanks, Shauna!)

Every person who holds the Position of Salesperson on your Organization Chart fills out a Salesperson Scorecard on a daily basis. If you hold the Position, even on an infrequent basis, you must play by the rules and fill out your Scorecard. As the owner, you lead by example.

Print a blank form for each Salesperson...one Scorecard per week. Every day, each Salesperson will fill out his or her score for that day. This form is filled out manually. This is essential. This "manual moment" ensures that the Salesperson confronts his or her performance. Right-stuff people like accountability. Sales-focused salespeople want to know the score and where they stand.

Note the Sales Goal and Close-Rate Goal boxes on the Salesperson Scorecard. Those Goals come from your budget. If you completed the Bare Bones Biz Budgeting spreadsheets, you can pull those Goals from your budget. If you completed the Baby Budget, use the Pricing Exercise from Day Thirteen to help you create your Daily and Weekly

Sales Goals. Individual Sales Goals come from dividing your total Sales Goals by the number of Salespeople on the team.

If you are not yet comfortable with your budget, skip the Goals columns for now and just start gathering the actual performance information. You can add that later. We'll remind you to do that in Week Six. Ultimately, sales performance must be measured against sales Goals.

Here's the best part about the Scorecards: You can identify those who need help...and help them. And you can identify those who are doing great and reward them.

Sales Training

If you are going to keep score, you must commit to helping people improve their scores. To keep score and not offer Sales Training is just mean. To offer Sales Training and not keep score...well, how will you know if your Sales Training is working?

The numbers on the Salesperson Scorecard are a reflection of the Salesperson's performance. The numbers are influenced by what he is doing, and how she is behaving with your customers. Are there behaviors that, if performed on each and every sales opportunity, would positively impact those numbers? Yes!

For instance, we know that Salespeople who develop personal relationships with their customers sell more than those who don't. What are a few behaviors that help create those relationships? Establishing eye contact, wearing a clean uniform, using polite speech and remembering to say "please" and "thank you." Sales Training is teaching behaviors that help Salespeople be more successful.

Perhaps you are already a great Salesperson. Or maybe you have some great Salespeople on your team. Formal Sales Training gives you and your team a common language with which you can speak, learn and teach good sales behaviors.

There is an endless supply of great Sales Training products on the market. Tomorrow's Coaching Lesson is about incorporating a formal Sales Training program into your company. It is an essential component of your sales management program.

Sales That Feel Good

As I mentioned yesterday, good sales feel good. Those are the only kind of sales to make. Understand that we are not interested in sales at any cost or using unethical techniques to deliver sales. Good sales feel good to you, your team and your customers. Stay focused on sales that feel good. Your sales efforts must support your Mission, your Vision and your Values.

Sales Meetings

Starting today, you are going to have a weekly Sales Meeting. Only positive, sales-focused topics are presented in this meeting. The intent: to recognize and celebrate Sales.

Ideas for Sales Meeting topics:

- Recap of great Sales performance from the previous week
- Sales Training sessions
- Elevator Speech practice
- Sales Contest results
- Recognize Top Sales.
- Introduce new products and services.
- Role Play sales situations.
- Share sales compliments from customers.
- Listen to a sales training tape, and then discuss.
- Read a chapter from a sales training book.
- Watch sales training videotapes.
- Invite "guest star" salespeople from other companies.

Make it fun! Good sales feel good…to customers and salespeople. The Sales Meeting should be a fun, safe, energizing gathering to honor good Sales and salesmanship. Enthusiastically applaud all efforts to share and participate in the activities and training. Limit the agenda to Sales only.

The Sales Meeting is NOT an arena for attacking your team for poor performance. As a general meeting rule, praise anywhere and everywhere, discipline in private. Keep the Sales Meeting upbeat and positive. (Next week you'll learn more about meetings in the *Getting it Done* section of The Bare Bone Biz Plan.)

The Salesperson Scorecards, Sales Training and Sales Meeting are three components of a comprehensive sales management program and will help you to develop the *Getting it Sold* section of your Bare Bones Biz Plan.

Exercise: Hold a Sales Meeting

Today, you will hold a Sales Meeting. Schedule an hour with your Salespeople.

Host this meeting even if the team includes just you and one other person. Act as if you have an army of salespeople, and you soon may.

- Let them know that their actual performance will impact your budget, the Sales Goals and Close-Rate Goals. Do your best to communicate how all areas of your

▶ TIP Like all my forms, you can customize the Salesperson Scorecard for your company. Incorporate your lingo and any Sales statistics unique to your business. Don't get fancy - keep it simple!

business are dependent on one another. You have been crafting your business plan to the best of your ability. Now you need their help, their data, to refine your budget and business plan.

- Let them know that by keeping score, you can help those who need help and reward those who are performing well.
- Share your intention to develop a bonus plan for exceeding sales Goals. To do that, you will need a month or two of Scorecard information and financial information.
- Announce your commitment to Sales Training. Ask for their sales program suggestions. (Tomorrow you will research your Sales Training program.)
- If you have personally struggled with salesphobia, share your story. Promise to help them get over any salesphobia that they may have.
- Wrap up with an announcement of the day and time for each week's Sales Meeting.

Plan to meet individually with each Salesperson to go over his or her Scorecard. You may discover some resistance. Suppose Rocco complains about the paperwork. Stand firm. It may be salesphobia rearing its ugly head. Let him know that you need this information and that you are committed to his success as a Salesperson.

Make sure each Salesperson understands the form and can demonstrate how to fill it out. Jot this reminder down in your Master To-Do List.

Each Salesperson should keep copies of his or her Scorecards to track progress. On Monday of each week, the person in charge of bookkeeping should assemble the updated Year To Date Scorecards. Keep the most current copy of this form in your Plan Binder in the *Getting it Sold* section.

Store a copy of your most recent Sales Meeting Agenda in your Plan Binder in the *Getting it Sold* Section. Congratulations on your progress toward establishing a sales management system at your company!

Sample Document Sales Meeting Agenda

Updated ____________

- ☐ Open with a reading of your Mission and your Vision.
- ☐ Deliver your Elevator Speech.
- ☐ Call on someone to give his or her Elevator Speech.
- ☐ Recap today's lesson. Let them know you are committed to their success and to creating a customer-focused, sales-focused culture.
- ☐ Introduce the Salesperson Scorecard.
- ☐ Pass out blank Scorecards and go over how to fill them out.

Sample Document Sales Scorecard

NAME: ______________________________

DAILY SALES GOAL: $______________

WEEKLY SALES GOAL: $ ______________

CLOSE RATE GOAL: %______________

FOR THE WEEK ENDING: ______________

Day	# of Sales Calls Run	# of Sales Calls Closed	Actual Close Rate (calls closed/calls run)	+ or - Close Rate Goal	Actual Sales	+ or – Sales Goal (Actual Sales – Sales Goal)	Average Invoice (Actual Sales/ Closed Calls)
Monday							
Tuesday							
Wednesday							
Thursday							
Friday							
Saturday							
Sunday							

Day 18

WEDNESDAY'S COACHING LESSON: SALES TRAINING BASICS

"We are all salesmen every day of our lives. We are selling our ideas, our plans, our enthusiasms to those with whom we come in contact."
~ Charles Schwab

As part of your business plan, you must outline the basic Sales Training program you will use to help your team make good sales. Sales Training is teaching people the skills they need to serve customers, help them solve their customers' problems and satisfy their needs. Review your Target Market and USP in the *Setting Sight* section of your Plan Binder. Sales Training is about building better behaviors so that you can deliver your USP. Sales Training is not a pep talk. We suggest you skip the pep talk! Confidence comes from one source: sales success. Teach your Salespeople skills to help them be successful.

On our Sample Organization Chart for See More Blinds, Inc., Suki is the Sales Manager. She is the one responsible for sales management, including Sales Training. As the owner of a sales-focused company, you would work closely with your Sales Manager to develop your Sales Training program.

Sales Training Basics

Your Sales Training program should include:

- Salesperson Scorecards
- A standard Sales Process
- Group training at your weekly Sales Meeting
- Seminars and workshops, local and out-of-town sales training events
- Individual coaching
- One-to-one meetings with each Salesperson to review his or her Scorecard and to work on sales-skill development
- Following the Salesperson in the field or in the shop to assess and improve performance

Let's address the Sales Process. The Sales Process is a description of the steps involved to transforming prospective customers into happy purchasers. You could create your own Sales Process. Our suggestion: Don't reinvent the wheel. Find a well-known professional sales trainer and "adopt" his or her program. Incorporate its language and Sales Process into your Sales Training Program.

Understand that this Sales Trainer is only required to visit your shop in the form of tapes, books and videos. You may choose to arrange for private consulting at your company, or to attend a live Sales Training session. However, it is not required. You are interested in the sales materials and the sales language. The "adopted" Sales Trainer supports your company's Sales Trainer: the Sales Manager.

The Sales Process

Every Sales Trainer will have a similar Sales Process. Here are the Bare-Bones Basics of every Sales Process:

- Opening. Greet the customer and establish a relationship.
- Discovery. Ask good questions and listen closely to the customer. Look for needs and wants.
- Problem solving. Present product and service options, and list the benefits to the customer. Share your USP.
- Closing. Ask for the sale...and the customer says "Yes!"
- Follow up. Reassure the customer about his or her purchase and offer additional products and services.

The Sales Process is what it is. However, each Sales Trainer has his take on the steps and makes it his own by naming them. The Opening step may be called the Greeting or the Introduction or Auditioning. The Discovery step might also be called Probing. The Sales Trainer may add sub-steps, such as Trial Close, Objection Handling and Close.

Adopt a Sales Trainer Exercise

Find a Sales Trainer and sales program to "adopt" for your company. Go to Barnes and Noble and look through the Sales Training section. Search for "sales training" on the Internet. Call your Board of Advisors and ask for their recommendations. Listen closely

The Frankenstein Factor

The main reason for adopting a Sales Trainer is that it will give you a standard language, a standard Sales Process. Without it, you may create a Frankenstein at your company. A Frankenstein describes a patched-together system that uses different names for the same things. A Frankenstein may include contradictory steps. It's confusing!

to recommendations from your team, particularly from high-producing Salespeople.

Do you belong to a progressive trade association in your industry? Find out what Sales Training programs your trade association offers. They might have a wonderful, industry-specific Sales Training program available as a member service.

Learn about different Sales Trainers. Read their books or listen to their tapes. You'll find much of their content is the same. Find one whose personality and philosophy align with your Mission, Vision and Values. The behaviors outlined in his or her Sales Process should be founded in basic good manners and respect. Pass on the programs with a tightly scripted sales pitch. Look for a program that focuses on good communication skills.

Be sure to "interview" a few of my favorite Sales Trainers:

- Tom Hopkins
- Brian Tracy
- Jim Rohn
- Mark Victor Hansen
- Dale Carnegie
- Al Levi
- Dennis Waitley
- Jeff Gitomer

The Most Important Sales Skill...is Listening!

Great Salespeople, no matter what sales system they use, always ask good questions and listen to the answers. Paul Swan is "The Listening Coach" and he is developing an audio program to help you become a better listener. We'll keep you posted and announce the release of this program at www.barebonesbiz.com.

Look into the product packages these trainers offer. Do they have books, tapes, CDs, videos, workbooks, and seminars available?

Then make the decision...and adopt a Sales Trainer.

Find the page called Sales Training Summary in this book. Fill it out, and insert this page in the *Getting it Sold* section of your Plan Binder. You might find a page from your adopted trainer's website or brochure that offers a brief summary of the program. Three-hole punch the page and place it in your Plan Binder.

Don't forget to adjust your budget for travel and education expenses.

So far this week, the focus has been Sales. You've learned the Bare-Bones Basics for creating a sales-management program and a sales-focused culture. Next, you'll turn your attention to Marketing.

Sample Document Sales Training Program Summary

Updated____________________

Who is your adopted Sales Trainer?

What Sales Training products and services are available to support this program?

Describe how you will deliver Sales Training to your Salespeople. Include products, services, time requirements, and dates.

Day 19

THURSDAY'S COACHING LESSON: BARE BONES MARKETING BASICS – PART 1 – BRANDING

Over the next two days, you'll learn the Bare-Bones Basics of branding, marketing and publicity. And you'll continue building the *Getting it Sold* section of your Plan Binder.

"Obstacles can't stop you. Problems can't stop you. Most of all, other people can't stop you. Only you can stop you."
~ Jeffrey Gitomer, Author

Brand and Demand

Marketing has a two-fold purpose:

- To build your brand
- To create demand for your products and services

Your brand consists of your name, your logo and your message. Branding is burning your name, logo and Unique Selling Proposition into the minds of every person in your market. Branding takes time, but it takes less time with a powerful brand. One that's easy to remember. One that associates your product with your customers' needs and wants. In the short run, you need customers demanding your products and services and creating sales now. Becoming a great marketer takes energy, passion and a willingness to experiment. A great marketer will do whatever needs to be done to get the phone ringing and the shop crowded.

A great brand will help customers remember you and call you when they are in the market for your products and services. A great brand will multiply the impact of your marketing dollars.

Great Brand Examples

At this company, the name, logo and message are all the same thing: Target. This is the place. Come right here. Buy this. Target sometimes doesn't even use words in its television commercials. But we understand...we should go there!

Check out www.1800gotjunk.com. The company name, logo, phone number and website address are the same. 1 800 Got Junk provides junk removal services. The brand is catching on. And in the short run, they get the phone ringing with television, billboard and radio ads. And publicity. Every morning, members of the team put on bright blue clown wigs, stand next to busy intersections and wave "1 800 Got

Roy Williams is brilliant at Branding. Check out www.wizardofads.com

Junk?" signs to passing motorists.

At Benjamin Franklin Plumbing, the Unique Selling Proposition is "the punctual plumber." Most folks don't expect a plumber to show up on time. In fact, Benjamin Franklin Plumbing promises, "If there's a delay, it's YOU we pay!" That gets customers' attention …and it assures them that they won't wait around all day for a plumber. That's a USP with real customer value.

Franchises and Branding

One of the best reasons to consider a franchise is the Brand. Every dollar every other franchisee spends on marketing leverages your brand. If you're considering buying a franchise, or if you'd like to franchise your business, explore the International Franchise Association at www.franchise.org

Brand Exam Exercise

Spend some time today reflecting on your name, logo and USP. You've been working on your Elevator Speech. If you have a great USP, you have the basis for a great Marketing program and a great brand.

Now, consider your name.

- Does it communicate your USP?
- Is it difficult to spell or pronounce?
- Does clever spelling keep people from finding it in the phone book?
- Does your name trigger good feelings about your company or your products?
- Does your name make your customers think of another company?
- Even if you are just starting your business, you have been calling it something. Should you run with what you have, or start over?
- What about your logo?
- Does it support your USP?
- Are the colors easy to print and reproduce?
- Do the colors create positive feelings?

- Is the design powerful and memorable?
- Can your customers see only your logo and recognize it as your company?

Here are the bare bones about your name, logo and USP: The passion you put into your Marketing and publicity efforts can overcome a less-than-perfect brand. There is no such thing as a perfect brand. Yet a great brand could become your most valuable asset.

You can make yourself nuts with this.

Set a time limit. Pick a future date on your calendar, no more than a month or two away. On that date, you will make a decision about your name, logo and USP. Between then and now, commit to learning about branding.

Today, spend an hour thinking about your brand and expanding your branding education. Consider the time, money and energy you will put into your branding strategy, and craft a plan.

And when that day shows up on your calendar, make a decision about your name, logo and USP. Commit to your brand. And run with it.

Test Your TOMA

If you have been in business a long time, you might check your TOMA before you change your name. TOMA stands for Top Of Mind Awareness, and it is a measure of the strength of your brand. T

TOMA, Inc., is a company that performs name awareness surveys. Its employees will call people in your market area and ask them to name a company who does what you do. For instance, "Name a fast food restaurant." Then they rank the results in order of strongest name awareness.

If 90% of the people in your market named your company in a TOMA survey about your industry, then stick with the name you are using. You are successfully branding your name into the minds of your customers and marketplace. If 2% name your company, you have little to lose by creating a new brand.

High TOMA survey scores are the result of a great brand and relentless marketing. Learn more about TOMA surveys by calling 800.597.9798.

Day 20

FRIDAY'S COACHING LESSON: BARE BONES MARKETING BASICS – PART 2 – THE MARKETING PROCESS

"The moment one definitely commits oneself, then Providence moves too. All sorts of things occur to help one that would never otherwise have occurred…unforeseen incidents, meetings, and material assistance, which no man could have dreamed would have come his way."
~ Johann Wolfgang von Goethe

Today, you'll learn the basic steps of the Marketing Process and start assembling your Marketing Calendar.

Here are the Bare-Bones Basics of the Marketing Process:

- **Assemble ideas.** List at least 101 ways to market and publicize your business on your Master To-Do List.
- **Research expenses.** Find out what it costs for Yellow Pages ads, radio, billboards, TV, newspaper, classified ads, printing services, etc., for prospective marketing vehicles.
- **Research your competitors.** Discover what they do well and poorly. Find out what they offer and how much they charge. Look for ways to be better, cleaner, nicer, smarter, faster, and more polite.
- **Review and revise your budget.** Assess your actual sales and expenses to budget. Adjust your budget and your marketing efforts for the best effect with the fewest dollars.
- **Assemble the Marketing Calendar.** Assign marketing vehicles to dates on the calendar.
- **Create your marketing vehicles.** Coordinate efforts with graphic artists, advertising sales representatives and printing companies. Check for USP, consistency in brand.
- **Launch your marketing vehicles.** Make sure they get out into the marketplace.
- **Leverage your marketing efforts with publicity.** Get positive attention for your company on the basis of your USP, your personality, your good deeds in the community.
- **Assess your marketing efforts.** Keep track of the results. Do more of what works and less of what doesn't.
- **Repeat the process.**

Like your adopted Sales Trainer, you may be well served to adopt a Marketing Coach. If I could pick one person to help create a Marketing Calendar, it would be Nancy Michaels. Check out Nancy's book, Off The Wall Marketing Ideas, and meet Nancy at www.growyourbusiness-network.com. She is the queen of low-cost, high-impact marketing and publicity.

Other great marketers to "interview":

- Seth Godin
- Harry Beckwith
- Jay Conrad Levinson
- Jack Trout
- Al Ries

Each of these marketing gurus has written handfuls of books on tried-and-true marketing and publicity techniques. Certainly a member of your Board of Advisors has a wealth of experiential marketing knowledge. Plan to meet with him or her to go over marketing strategies and advertising purchasing strategies. And brainstorm with your most creative employees, friends and family members.

In my experience, the idea-generating portion of the process is easy. It tends to bog down when it comes to assembling the Marketing Calendar and executing the plan.

Marketing Calendar Exercise

Find the form called Marketing Calendar in this book or find a downloadable, customizable version of the form in The Complete Suite on the Buy Stuff page at www.barebones-biz.com.

In the *Making Money* section of your Plan Binder, refer to your budget. If you are using the Baby Budget, take note of the dollar amount you have budgeted for Marketing. If you are using the Bare Bones Biz Basic Budgeting Program, open the Excel file on your computer. Note the Marketing page. Refine your marketing budget numbers as you craft your Marketing Calendar. Make sure that they are in sync with each other.

Note that the Bare Bones Biz Basic Budgeting Program calculates the number of opportunity calls (sales leads) you need to generate. As you get more experiential knowledge about marketing, you'll be able to estimate how many calls a particular marketing vehicle can contribute to the total. Until you have that kind of data, you'll have to experiment.

Today, spend some time filling out the Marketing Calendar. Review the ideas on your Master To-Do List. Move your best ideas to the Marketing Calendar. Plug in the dollars required. It's an engineering challenge...how to best use your marketing dollars for maximum effect. Make sure you cross-reference your budget with the Marketing Calendar. Note that you will check your successes by updating the Marketing Calendar every week. The person on the Organization Chart in charge of Marketing is responsible for keeping the Marketing Calendar current.

There's Always Room for Publicity.

No matter what your budget is, there is always room for publicity-generating items on your Marketing Calendar.

Positive publicity is when someone other than you says wonderful things about your company to your customers or your community.

Negative publicity is when someone says bad things about you to your customers or your community. Not to worry! Negative publicity can be your best-ever opportunity to communicate how wonderful you are to the world. We'll explore this in the *Making Sure* section of The Bare Bones Biz Plan.

Add publicity-generating efforts to each week of your Marketing Calendar.

Even if you have not yet committed to your brand, you can spend time working on the Marketing Process. Start putting together your Marketing Calendar. Keep the most current version of your Marketing Calendar in the *Getting it Sold* section of your Plan Binder. Remember to update your budget and insert the latest version in the *Making Money* section of the Plan Binder.

Your Weekend Homework

Practice what you've learned this week by selling your spouse or significant other…on YOU. What's great about you? What's your personal USP? Reflect on your Mission and Vision for this relationship.

Learn about your Target Market. What needs are being met? What wants are not being addressed? Ask good questions and listen to the answers.

What marketing vehicles would be most effective? A billboard? A personal, handwritten note? How can you best present the benefits of YOU? Dancing? Bowling?

Here's to closing the sale this weekend!

Consistent Image or Circus Train?

Put up a corkboard in your office to be used exclusively for displaying your marketing vehicles. You'll be able to tell if your Yellow Page ads, newspaper ads, flyers, postcards, etc., are working together to build a clear, consistent brand. You can check the consistency of color and production quality. Remember, however, the most important element of a marketing vehicle is: Did it generate leads and sales? Track the performance of each effort in your Marketing Calendar.

Sample Document Marketing Calendar

updated _______

When	What	Expense	Calls Generated	Expense Per Call	Sales $	Expense to Total Sales	Repeat?
Aug 8-14	YP AD	$350					
Aug 15-21	YP AD	$350					
Aug 22-24	YP AD	$350					
Aug 29-Sept 4	YP AD	$350					

Week
Five:
Getting
it Done!

Day 21

MONDAY'S COACHING LESSON: THE TOOLS FOR GETTING IT DONE

"The Presidency is a decision-making job."
~ William Jefferson Clinton

Today you'll learn about the tools in The Bare Bones Biz System for *Getting it Done. Getting it Done* means delivering your wonderful products and services to your customers so that their needs are met and their problems solved. *Getting it Done* means consistently delivering your USP so well that your customers are delighted by their experience and will come back for more. *Getting it Done* means delivering on your promises...to yourself, your team and your customers. *Getting it Done* means focused activity in the direction of your Goals, Mission and Vision.

Today, we'll review the forms and checklists we've already introduced and show you how they flow together to move you in the direction of your Mission, Vision and Goals.

Urgent vs. Important

Business philosopher Stephen Covey, author of First Things First, says our activities can be categorized as Urgent or Not Urgent and Important or Not Important.

	Urgent	Not Urgent
Important	**Quadrant I** Crisis Deadline-driven projects	**Quadrant II** Planning Preparation Recharging activities
Not Important	**Quadrant III** Interruptions Some meetings Some phone calls Mail, e-mail	**Quadrant IV** Trivia Excessive TV Time wasters Escape activities

► **TIP** Add Stephen Covey's book *First Things First* to your MUST READ list!

Stephen's research has shown that the highest-performing companies spend 65% to 80% of their time in Quadrant II activities.

The time you've been spending working on your Plan Binder and crafting your business plan is Quadrant II time. If you don't purposefully commit to spending the time in Quadrant II, Quadrants I, III and IV will take over your day. And the problem is that if you don't spend energy on the Important, Not Urgent planning tasks, you'll never resolve the systemic problems that cause you to waste so much time "putting out fires" or just "escaping" after an exhausting day.

From "Big Thinking" to Focused Activities

Today's exercise is assembling your Top Projects list. We'll start with a brief overview of your Plan Binder to help you see how the work you have been doing in The Bare Bones Biz Plan helps you answer this question:

"What should I focus on doing NOW to achieve my Goals?"

Business guru Stephen Covey says, "Begin with the end in mind." That's why you started this adventure by developing your Mission, Target Market, Vision, USP and Values statements.

Next, I asked you to write down your Goals. Goals are "to have" statements. Goals are measurable and achievable. Goals should be written down and have a date attached to them. Goals are the milestones in the pursuit of your Mission and your Vision. The *Setting Sight* exercises provide the boundaries of your business plan.

- You created the Organization Chart and Position Descriptions to help you start Building Your Team.
- In the Making Money section, you developed your Budget to support your financial Goals.
- You spent time creating your Sales Scorecards and Marketing Calendar in the Getting it Sold section.

Note how the sections flow from one to the other. Understand the importance of integrating each section of your plan so that it supports the whole.

Throughout, I've been encouraging you to write down any ideas, to do's and projects on your Master To-Do List. The Master To Do List keeps you from losing track of the things that need to be done to build your business.

By now, your Master To-Do List may be a very long list!

So...what to do first? What should you focus on doing NOW to achieve your Goals?

Top Projects List Exercise

Find the Top Projects form at the end of this section. The Top Project List can help you get things done and keep you from being overwhelmed. The Top Projects are the FEW projects that you and your team will FOCUS on NOW to help you accomplish your Goals.

Look over the "A" priority Goals on the Goal sheet. What actions, projects, to do's will help you accomplish those Goals? The items on your Master To-Do List may inspire you as to what needs to be done to move you to your Goals.

Remember the saying, "How do you eat an elephant?" The answer is, of course, "One bite at a time."

The next question may be, "Where do I start?"

The answer: "It really doesn't matter!"

What should your Top 10 Projects be? Gather input from your team. Justify each one by asking: Is this moving us toward our Goals? Is this project helping us make more sales? Is this the best use of our time and energy at this moment?

Examples of Top Projects can be…

- Completing your Marketing Calendar for the next six months
- Developing Procedures for the Salespeople
- Creating your Position Descriptions
- Revising your Budget for this year

Would you like help from your team as to what to put on the Top Projects List? Ask for their help. But the final decision is yours. Put no more than 10 projects on the Top Projects list. For another project to make it to the Top Projects list, one project has to get done and moved off the list.

Tomorrow, we'll address using the Top Projects List to focus your meetings…and Get it Done!

Store a copy of your Top Projects list in the *Getting it Done* section of your Plan Binder.

If your idea of a time-management system is a pencil and a Post-it pad, you may get bogged down in this section. Do yourself a favor…attempt to use the tools we offer in this section.

The best part about the Top Project List? It helps you move out of overwhelm and into focused action. It's a nice feeling!

Day 22

TUESDAY'S COACHING LESSON: MEETING BASICS

Today, you'll learn the Bare-Bones Basics for making meetings powerful and effective Quadrant II events.

"The world must learn to work together, or finally it will not work at all."
~ Dwight D. Eisenhower

Meet With Yourself First

Make a standing appointment with yourself to review and update your Plan Binder and structure your Personal Calendar. Pick an hour on Sunday night or Monday morning, before the work week begins. Commit to this meeting! Whether you are just getting started in business or you are the CEO of General Electric, this meeting with yourself is the most important meeting of the week.

Invest the hour reviewing your business plan and organizing your upcoming week. Flip through your Plan Binder. Update the forms and reports. Keep only current and relevant information in your Plan Binder. File or throw away the outdated pages.

Read over your Perfect Life for inspiration. Look over your Mission and Vision. See yourself achieving your Goals. Review the Top Projects List and the Master To-Do List. Edit and refine your Plan Binder.

Ask yourself, "This week, what is the BEST use of my time?"

Your time is infinitely valuable. Spend it wisely. Don't squander it. Time management guru Dan Sullivan says, "You can have everything you love in life as long as you give up things you hate."

Don't do things you hate. Don't hang out with people who suck the life out of you. You are too smart for that! Life is too precious.

Commit your time to things that make you happy with people you love, do things that move you to your Goals and allow you to express your greatest gifts. Plan your week to reflect your Perfect Life.

Block out time for your activities this week on your Personal Calendar. You can use a standard week-at-a-glance calendar. Or you can…

Brighten Your Outlook

If you are parked at your desk for most of your workday, you might consider using Microsoft Outlook for your Personal Calendar. More

"It has been computed by some political arithmetician that, if every man and woman would work for four hours each day on something useful, labor would provide sufficient to procure all the necessities and comforts of life, want and misery would be banished out of the world, and the rest of the 24 hours might be leisure and pleasure."
~ Benjamin Franklin

than likely, Outlook is already loaded on your computer. Outlook is not the same as Outlook Express. Outlook Express is primarily an e-mail management program. For the Outlook program, look for a camouflage-green clock icon. If you don't have Outlook, you can preview or download it from www.microsoft.com.

Set the Outlook Calendar to display all seven days from left to right. Go to Tools, Options, Calendar Options…and click on all seven days.

Now, plan your week.

Let this be your mantra: What is the BEST use of my time?

Block out family commitments first. Look ahead for upcoming travel and meetings. Schedule time to fulfill the Responsibilities for each Position you hold on the Organization Chart. Block out time to work on your Top Projects. If you don't make time for the Non-Urgent yet Important stuff, it just won't get done. You can always click and drag and reschedule.

When you schedule an appointment in Outlook, check out the label feature. You can color-code your appointments. I use green for personal/family appointments. Currently, writing this book is on my Top Project list. I coded my scheduled writing time in purple. If I intend to finish the project on time, there better be enough purple on the Outlook Calendar.

Keep just one calendar. Otherwise, you may miss your kid's game because you wrote it on the calendar on the kitchen wall but you didn't record it in your Calendar.

Invest in a Treo®, iPhone® or BlackBerry®. These tools can be synched with your computer's Outlook files so that you can take your Calendar, your e-mail and your contact information with you.

During the week, keep the Master To-Do List handy. Use it to write down anything you need to remember. At your Sunday night or Monday morning meeting, transfer phone numbers, appointments, etc. from the Master To-Do List into Outlook.

As you progress through your week, Outlook will help you hold yourself accountable. All day long, my Outlook reminds me of appointments, meetings, project times, and phone calls. The key is spending that hour Sunday night or Monday morning to set yourself up for a highly productive week.

Meeting With a Group

Here are the Bare-Bones Basics for effective meetings with team members.

> *"Give a hard job to a lazy man to find an easy way to get it done."*
> ~ Jim Hamilton

- By invitation only. Require only the people who need to be at the meeting to attend.
- Be prepared and start on time. Ending early is fine.
- Name your meetings. This clarifies the topic and who is required to attend. Have fun with this. You could call your Sales Meeting the Sales Jamboree or the Safety Meeting the Look Out Meeting.
- Never discipline in a group setting. It's insulting to the people to whom the lecture does not apply and it dilutes the message for those to whom the lecture is directed.
- Make sure each group meeting has some love! Celebrate wins, educational achievements, sales Goals met, compliments from customers, birthdays and new babies.
- Have an agenda and stick to it. Hold short and sweet meetings on focused topics. Don't try to address everything at one meeting. Discuss sales at the Sales Meeting and new payroll procedures at a Payroll Meeting. One point well taken beats many points presented.

Meeting One-to-One

Meet weekly with every person on the Organization Chart who reports to you. Go over his Scorecard. Review her progress on projects. Work together to solve challenges. Let them know how much you appreciate them. Keep these meetings to 15 minutes.

- In a small company, be sure to touch base informally with every employee every week.
- Address any problems individually and immediately.

Six-foot-four-inch Abe Lincoln was asked once, "How long should a man's legs be?" He replied, "Long enough to reach the ground." Your meetings should be long enough to communicate what needs to be communicated but no longer.

Everyone must bring his or her Personal Calendar to every meeting. Each person is responsible for recording his own assignments and synchronizing her Calendar.

Find the Meeting Agenda form in this book, or download the customizable form at www.barebonesbiz.com. It's included in *The Complete Suite* on the Buy Stuff page. Use a Meeting Agenda for every group meeting and for any one-to-one meeting with multiple topics. Keep upcoming meeting agendas in the appropriate section of your Plan Binder.

Plan Your Meetings Exercise: Part One

Today, schedule a group meeting to go over your Top Projects with the appropriate team members. Complete a Meeting Agenda form in preparation for this meeting.

At the meeting, present your Top Projects List. Delegate the Top Projects. Discuss what it will take to complete the projects, and schedule follow-up meetings. Make sure each team member records his or her own to do's. Set due dates.

Be sure to thank them for their time. Let them know you anticipate the successful, on-time completion of their projects and to do's.

Plan Your Meetings Exercise: Part Two

Spend some time today learning about Outlook. Snoop around. Play with the features. Look through the tutorial and help screens.

Schedule a recurring appointment for your Sunday night or Monday morning meeting. Schedule another for your Sales Meeting.

Congratulations! Now you are committed to *Getting it Done.*

► **TIP** Your actions should be in concert with your Mission, Vision and Values. Focus on activities that are interesting, fun and productive. It feels great to move in the direction of your Perfect Life. If your Projects inspire you, you are more likely to get them done!

Sample Document Meeting Agenda

Date and Start Time:______________________

Meeting Name/Topic :____

Who needs to attend?

Points of discussion:

____ Time ______

____ Time ______

____ Time ______

____ Time ______

____ Time ______

____ Time ______

____ Time ______

____ Time ______

End Time:_________

Points that came up that we can include in a future meeting:

Day 23

WEDNESDAY'S COACHING LESSON: CREATING YOUR PROCEDURES

"I'm working to improve my methods, and every hour I save is an hour added to my life."
~ Ayn Rand

Today you will learn how to create Procedures for your growing business. Take a look at the Position Descriptions you created in Week Two – *Building the Team*. Note the list of Responsibilities for each Position.

Remember, responsibilities are WHAT to do. Procedures are HOW to do it. For each Responsibility, you will create the Procedures for *getting it done.*

Procedures keep you from wasting time and energy on the small stuff. Have you ever spent half a day tracking down a part that you should have had on hand? Have you ever had to make an emergency trip to the store because you ran out of toilet paper in the office restroom? Procedures handle the "housekeeping" so that you and your team are free to serve and to sell!

Also, are you certain that each member of your installation team has the same installation standards? Procedures help you consistently deliver your USP. And Procedures help you grow your company.

Who Writes the Procedures?

The team member who holds the Position should write the Procedures for that Position, then submit the Procedures to his or her manager for review. Work with your team to develop Procedures for every area of your company. Ultimately, you will have a Procedure for just about everything that you do.

Writing the Procedures can be as simple as documenting what team members are currently doing. Work together with your team to discover the best practices within your group. The process will help you find the "holes" in your current systems…and fill them. Throughout the process, ask, "How does this Procedure support sales and service to our customers, now and in the future?"

If a Procedure is dependent on more than one team member's performance, have them partner up and work on their Procedures together. For instance, at See More Blinds, Inc., Suki and Pete should discuss how to communicate to customers when the sales process ends and the installation work begins. They can craft their Procedures to dovetail with each other.

A word of caution: This assignment can feel threatening to an insecure employee. Take the time to explain what you are doing and why. Assure each team member that you are building a company free of "housekeeping" headaches so that everyone is free to do his or her job better. To do that, you need to create Procedures - documents that explain "how things are done around here" - and you need their help.

Build "Checks" into the Procedures

"Checks" are points in the Procedure where another person or another Procedure verifies the work or information. For instance, in the Deposit Procedure, have the manager or owner verify the cash and sign off on the deposit. Without "checks," you put good people under suspicion if something goes wrong. Your team will help you create a system that "checks" and protects them.

Build a Procedure Exercise

Today, you will work on building Procedures for your company. Work with one of your team members. Select one of the Responsibilities in his or her Position and create a Procedure for *getting it done.* Start with how he or she is currently handling that Responsibility and go from there.

Note the example on the Procedure form. Find the form in this book, or download the customizable version at www.barebonesbiz.com. It's part of The Complete Suite on the Buy Stuff page.

Fill out the Procedure form with each step necessary to handle the Responsibility. Some Responsibilities may require more than one Procedure. That's fine.

Be as detailed as you can. This will save you time in the long run. Build at least one Procedure today. Store a copy of the Procedure in the appropriate section of your Plan Binder. And make sure the team member who will use the Procedure has a copy.

Make an Appointment on your Outlook calendar to follow up. Find out....Does the Procedure work? Are there some steps missing? How can it be improved? What can you do to make it better?

Remember, this Plan Binder is a work in process. You can always modify and add to the Position Descriptions and Procedures. Let your team know that you are always interested in making things easier, better, faster, and more professional.

Sample Document See More Blinds and Window Coverings, Inc. Procedure

Updated: ___________

Division: Getting it Sold

Position: In Charge of Publicity and Marketing

Responsibility: Keep the customer service area clean.

Behaviors: Every work day, by 9 a.m...

- ☐ Remove all trash from the area.
- ☐ Take one 55-gallon trash bag from the box on the floor of the storage closet.
- ☐ Empty all wastebaskets into the trash bag. Wastebaskets are located:
- ☐ To the left of the front door.
- ☐ Under the Customer Service Representative's desk.
- ☐ Put the trash bag in the dumpster at the north end of the parking lot.
- ☐ Clean all windows, inside and out.
- ☐ Use Windex. The Windex is kept on the third shelf of the storage closet.
- ☐ Use clean paper towels. The paper towels are on the second shelf of the storage closet.
- ☐ Wipe down all countertops.
- ☐ Use the wood soap spray. The wood soap spray is kept on the third shelf of the storage closet.
- ☐ Use clean paper towels. The paper towels are on the second shelf of the storage closet.
- ☐ Vacuum the floor.
- ☐ Find the vacuum hose in the storage closet.
- ☐ Connect the hose to the central vac outlet on the south wall. (See diagram)
- ☐ Turn the vacuum on by flipping the switch on the main unit to the ON position.
- ☐ The main vacuum unit is the black box on the right wall of the storage closet.

Training Tip for Crazy Family Businesses!

If you are working in a family business, written Procedures can keep you from killing each other. She may be your mom, but if she is in charge of bookkeeping at your company, she needs to create and follow Procedures. You might end up firing her! Keep your emotions in check and stay focused on doing the right things to achieve your Mission and realize your Vision. Create Procedures and hold everyone accountable. Al Levi of Appleseed Business developed his first-rate management skills in his family's business. He worked with his dad, brothers and sister to put together Procedures for every area of their super-successful service and energy company. And they still speak to each other! Meet Al and check out his site at www.appleseedbusiness.com. He has great ideas for building your Procedures.

Day 24 THURSDAY'S COACHING LESSON: BARE BONES TRAINING BASICS

"You can have whatever you want in life if you help enough other people get what they want."
~ Zig Ziglar

Today, you'll learn Bare Bones Training Basics. Generally speaking, the better your training program, the less skilled your prospective employees need to be. In other words, the more training you do, the more choices you have when it comes to building your team…and getting things done.

Consider the U.S. Marine Corps. Its slogan: We're looking for a few good men. Notice that the Marines don't require candidates to have weapons-handling experience, foreign language skills or be in excellent physical condition. They are looking for good people, and they train those people to the USMC standards to do all kinds of specialized tasks.

If you don't have a formal training program, then you must depend on finding employees who already know how to do the job you are offering. That really reduces your hiring choices. Also, you can be put into the uncomfortable position of being held hostage by your employees.

> *"Oh, I can't lose Jody! She is the only qualified high-temperature deep-fryer operator we have! I'll just pretend I didn't notice that she came to work 45 minutes late."*

You are not living up to your Values when you lower your standards. Your integrity is on the line. Everything you have worked on in The Bare Bones Biz Plan is designed to help you raise the standards to which you hold yourself and your employees. You are looking for a few good men and women. You can train them.

Level One and Level Two Training

- **Level One** is the training you provide so that team members can perform their assigned Procedures to the minimum acceptable level. Level One Training ends when your employee can perform the Procedure well enough to be held accountable for it.
- **Level Two** is the training you provide to enhance your employees' skills and abilities beyond the minimum levels. Level Two Training is for increasing performance and efficiency.

For example: You could teach me how to make a basketball freethrow. I could learn what line to stand behind and which hoop to aim for when I throw the ball. That's Level One training on the Procedure. I could "sign off" on that after a few minutes of training.

To get good at shooting freethrows, I would work on my technique. I may need to try holding the ball in different ways. I may do some specialized weight training. I may need to practice shooting the ball 50 times in a row. That's Level Two Training.

Depending on the Procedure, you decide whether or not to offer Level Two Training. For instance, the Procedure for turning on the restaurant lights requires no additional training. When it comes to selling Procedures, however, a Salesperson is well served by continuing with Level Two Training...forever!

Start by *making sure* all your team members are trained on the Procedure basics – Level One. Then add the Level Two Training.

The Training Process

These are the Bare-Bones basic steps of the Training Process. The process is the same for Level One and Level Two Training.

- **"I'll do it."** As the trainer, explain and demonstrate the Procedure. Use easy-to-understand words. You can do the Procedure yourself, draw a diagram to illustrate it or show a movie of the Procedure. Try more than one approach. Refer to the written Procedure as you go.
- **"Now you do it."** Ask your trainee to demonstrate the behaviors and duplicate the Procedure. Take as much time as you need to make sure that he or she can perform the Procedure and explain the reasons for doing it.
- **Role play.** Now act it out together. Take turns playing the customer. This will help you both see how the Procedure serves the customer and helps you deliver your USP. Role play is a dress rehearsal before the actual performance.
- **Real world.** Send your trainee out into the world. Observe the required behaviors in real time...at the shop, on the sales floor or in the field.
- **Sign off.** "Sign off" on the Procedure when you and your trainee are both comfortable with his or her understanding of the Procedure and the ability to perform it. Both of you will initial and date the Procedure. File a copy in his or her employee file.

Use the "sign off" to mark the end of the Training Process. As people learn new skills, make sure they are acknowledged...with a handshake, with a diploma or with a standing ovation at your next company meeting. Mary Kay Ash, founder of Mary Kay Cosmetics, understood that people are hungry for praise. Her company has grown to multibillion-dollar sales by praising the representatives for every accomplishment along the way. From personal notes to diamond rings to pink Cadillacs, Mary Kay showers her team with rewards for good performance.

Expand Your Training Offerings

Ask your employees, "What can we do to help you be more successful?" and incorporate their training suggestions. Here are some ideas for expanding your training program.

- Remember to adopt a Sales Trainer as we discussed in Week Four.
- Work with your product manufacturers for technical and product knowledge training.
- Ask your insurance agent to sponsor a safety program.
- Offer English as a second language classes.
- Offer personal finance and debt-reduction classes.
- Offer smoking-cessation or weight-loss programs.

Level One Training "Sign Off" and Accountability

Once an employee has signed off on a Procedure, something really wonderful happens. The team member is now responsible for *getting it done*. Accountability begins. From the point of the sign off, any failure to perform the Procedure is not a lack of training, but a lack of willingness. While he or she may improve skills through Level Two Training, as of the Level One sign-off, he or she is expected to perform the behaviors to acceptable standards and should be held accountable.

You have the right and the responsibility to require team members to play the game your way. Hold them accountable. Good people like accountability. Tomorrow we'll address getting the right people on the bus and the wrong people off the bus.

Measure the effectiveness of your training by tracking performance and by reviewing the Scorecards. Do the numbers improve? Are you reaching your Goals? Are team members performing the Procedures as intended? Does the training program support your Mission, Vision and Values? If so, you know you are on the right training track!

Level One Training Exercise

Select a team member for this exercise. Go through the Training Process with at least one Procedure. First, you take the trainer role. Then reverse roles. Let your employee be the trainer and you can be the trainee. This exercise is complete when you are both signed off on the Procedure.

Be sure to give each other a hearty handshake and congratulations! As Dale Carnegie says, "Show appreciation!"

Now you have the company structure to help the people on your team to be successful. You are building the foundation for the company of your dreams and are moving closer to your Perfect Life. However, the best part of building a great business may be the positive impact you can have on the lives of your team members.

Reflect on your experiences and jot your thoughts down in your Journal.

Day 25 FRIDAY'S COACHING LESSON: THE RIGHT PEOPLE TO GET IT DONE

"Hire smart. Train hard. Manage easy."
~ George Barnett

Over the past five weeks, you have made significant changes in your life and in your company. Not all of your employees are going to like these changes. It may be time to change the people on the bus.

In Week Two – *Building the Team* – you started your recruiting efforts. Consistent recruiting in advance of your hiring needs can provide a choice of good candidates who are willing and want to work for your company.

Today you will spend time thinking about your team. Who are the right people to have on the bus? Is there someone who needs to get off the bus? We sabotage our efforts to build a team because of our misunderstanding of teamwork. A team is a result of individual efforts in the pursuit of a mutual Goal. The Goal: great sales and service to your customers.

Rewarding Poor Performance

Mark Victor Hansen says, "That which you recognize, you energize." If you reward poor performance, you will have more poor performance. Have you ever given someone a raise in the hopes that you will improve his lackluster performance? Have you ever given a bonus to someone who didn't deserve one because "she tried."

Have you ever ignored a high-performing individual to spend countless hours trying to get minimum performance out of an underachiever? Are there family members taking up space on the bus because the politics of firing them are too much for you to bear?

Even worse, sometimes we punish great performance. I've seen this time and time again in sales. As soon as someone is really winning, management will split the territory or pinch the commission. After all, you can't have someone making too much money. It will make others –managers and under-performing salespeople – feel bad. Right? WRONG!

Firing, Hiring and Basic Human Resources Help

Fair, Square & Legal: Safe Hiring, Managing & Firing Practices to Keep You & Your Company Out of Court, by Donald H. Weiss, will help you develop Procedures for bringing people on the bus and getting them off the bus. Keep this book as a handy reference for the person in charge of Human Resources at your company.

Building the Right Team to Get it Done!

Remember, the key to your success is solving problems for your customers and making them happy. It's about great sales and service.

If you want good performance, then reward good performance.

If you are just starting your business, you have a wonderful opportunity to be selective in hiring. You have created great systems in your company. Hang on to your Plan Binder. As you grow and need help, you are much better prepared to welcome a new team member than you were five weeks ago, aren't you?

The People on the Bus Exercise: Part One

Review your Organization Chart. Think about every person and his or her Position(s) on the team. Of course, lying, cheating and stealing are always grounds for immediate dismissal.

Review each employee's performance. Ask these questions:

- Do your customers compliment or complain about him? Disney, Inc., has a zero-tolerance policy for customer complaints. One complaint is grounds for dismissal.
- Is he completing his assigned Top Projects on time?
- Is she performing at or above Goals on her Scorecard?
- Does he meet his Responsibilities and perform his assigned Procedures?
- Is she willing to play the game your way?
- Does she prioritize service and sales to your customers?

It's time to get the wrong people off the bus. You know who needs to go. It is not OK to decide to fire someone and continue to keep him or her on the payroll. Once you have made your decision, act on it. You dishonor the people on your team who share your Mission and are willing to do what it takes to get things done for your customers when you continue to employ a non-performer.

This exercise won't take very much time. It is better to do the work yourself than to have the wrong person doing it. Don't keep someone on until you find someone else. Let them go.

Notice how written Procedures and Scorecards can take the emotion out of your decision. When you have performance data, you and your employees always know where they stand. When you keep score, letting someone go won't come as a surprise.

When you let someone go, meet with each employee and tell them all that you made changes in the team. Let the person know you honor and respect him or her. Promise that you will find and hire "right stuff" people to help you in the pursuit of your Mission,

Vision, Goals and Values. Thank them for their help.

"No matter what we feel or know, no matter what our potential gifts or talents, only action brings them to life. Many of us understand concepts such as commitment, courage and love, but we truly KNOW only when we can DO. Doing leads to understanding, and action turns knowledge to wisdom." ~ Dan Millman

The People on the Bus Exercise: Part Two

By working The Bare Bones Biz Plan, you will know when you are ready to hire someone and for what Position. Doublecheck your budget. Are you ready?

Spend some time today developing your Hiring Procedures. If you let someone go today, promise yourself that you will use these Procedures to make better hiring choices in the future.

Take a look at the Hiring Checklist form in this book. You can download this customizable form at www.barebonesbiz.com. Look for it in The Complete Suite on the Buy Stuff page.

Spend some time thinking about and working on Procedures for the Hiring Process. You'll need Procedures for Interviews and your testing program, to include in the Employee Manual.

However, your Hiring Procedures don't have to be "finished" before you hire someone. Just having a checklist is 100% more Procedure than you used to have! If you are ready to hire someone, start the Hiring Process and do your best with the Procedures you have now. Review the Recruiting Checklist you started in Week Two – *Building the Team*. You can start the Hiring Process with the prospective team members you have listed.

Stay true to your Mission and Vision and live by your Values. Work diligently in the direction of your Goals. Stay focused on serving your customers and solving their problems. Be passionate about making a positive difference in the world. You will attract the right team members like a magnet.

Your Weekend Homework

Keep your meeting with yourself Sunday night or Monday morning. At that meeting, reflect on your *Setting Sight* pages and assess your progress towards your highest purpose and Perfect Life. Revisit each section of the Plan Binder. Think about each area of your business. Review your Top Projects List. Congratulate yourself for getting a few of them done.

As you plan your week, block out half a day to work on your Hiring Procedures. Update your Outlook Calendar and review the Top Projects List. Jot down thoughts and insights in your Journal.

Congratulations! Your business plan is up and running. You are making progress... and *getting it done*! Next week...*Making Sure*...

Sample Document Hiring Checklist

Updated____________

Name ____

Position ____

- ☐ Application completed Date _____ Manager's initials _____
- ☐ Flag page completed Date _____ Manager's initials _____
- ☐ First phone Interview Date _____ Manager's initials _____
- ☐ First in person Date _____ Manager's initials _____

Continue Yes or No?

- ☐ Skills test Date _____ Manager's initials _____
- ☐ Drug-free test Date _____ Manager's initials _____
- ☐ Background check Date _____ Manager's initials _____

Continue Yes or No?

- ☐ Second interview Date _____ Manager's initials _____

Hire? Yes or No?

- ☐ Offer accepted Date _____ Manager's initials _____
- ☐ Uniform ordered Date _____ Manager's initials _____
- ☐ Employee manual Date _____ Manager's initials _____
- ☐ Orientation complete Date _____ Manager's initials _____

www.BareBonesBiz.com
877.629.7647

Day 26 MONDAY'S COACHING LESSON: THE POWER OF CLARITY

"The progress is made by correcting the mistakes resulting from the making of progress."
~ Sir Claude Gibb

Welcome to Week Six of The Bare Bones Biz Plan. Hurray for you! This week is all about *making sure*. *Making sure* that you are on a good path and fulfilling your highest purpose. *Making sure* that your employees are doing a great job and that you are providing well for them. And today, we'll focus on *making sure* your customers are delighted by what you do for them.

Review your Unique Selling Proposition. Say your Elevator Speech out loud. Ask these questions:

- Are your products and services really what your customers need and want?
- Are your products and services being delivered in a consistently excellent way?
- How can you make sure?

Ask Your Customers

Your customers are happy to tell you what you can do to improve...if you ask them. Most business owners are just not interested in finding out whether or not their customers are happy. Perhaps they are afraid of finding out that they are not on the right track. They would rather not know, so they continue complaining about the economy, their employees and their customers!

But not you! You want to know. You want to grow and get better and better. So...ask your customers how you can serve them better.

Do you have a close friend who is also your customer? Is this friend a tell-it-like-it-is person? Good. Call him up. Let him know you want feedback about your services. Ask, "How are we doing? What could we do better? What are we missing?" Then listen. Don't interrupt or judge or comment. Just listen and jot down what he says in your Journal.

Send a thank-you note for the valuable feedback.

Other ways to ask your customer are...

- Follow-up phone calls. Ask, "Are you delighted with your purchase today?"

- Mail-back postcard report cards. Be sure to pay for the postage.
- On-the-store-floor surveys. Be creative. Ask, "If you could snap your fingers and have just what you are looking for, what would it be?"

And throughout the Sales Process...ask and LISTEN.

"Nothing in the world can take the place of persistence. Talent will not; nothing is more common than unsuccessful men with talent. Genius will not; unrewarded genius is almost a proverb. Education will not; the world is full of educated derelicts. Persistence and determination alone are omnipotent."
~ Calvin Coolidge

Get In on the Action

The next time you go to a restaurant, see if you spot the manager. A good restaurant manager will use the M.B.W.A. management system: Managing By Walking Around. While an M.B.W.A. manager may not look like she is doing much, she can be anticipating potential problems and averting them, or pitching in when an extra set of hands will keep things moving. She can catch someone doing something right and acknowledge him.

In your shop, get out there and walk around. Find out what's going on in your business. Watch the interaction between your customers and your employees. Think of it like this: On Game Day, the coach is on the field with his players, not locked in his office. Start M.B.W.A. today.

> *"His cardinal mistake is that he isolates himself, and allows nobody to see him; and by which he does not know what is going on in the very matter he is dealing with."*
> ~ Abraham Lincoln's reason for relieving General John C. Fremont from his command in Missouri, September 9, 1861

Ride Along

President Lincoln wrote these words to the man he was appointing to replace General Fremont. The new General would make no mistake about what was required of him: Get out there and circulate among the troops.

In a home service company, you won't know whether or not your customers are delighted with your services if you don't go out into the field. So get out there! By riding along, you have a wonderful opportunity to bond with your servicepeople. You can find out if your Procedures are actually helping create good sales and service or getting in the way. You can find out what kind of training may be needed to help your servicepeople improve their skills. You won't know...unless you go.

Mystery Shopping

If you are serious about excellent customer service, you'll implement a Mystery Shopping program. Mystery Shopping is a technique for testing customer service. Here is how it works: A Mystery Shopper will go to your business and...shop. Or you can arrange to have a Mystery Shopper call and schedule service at her home. A Mystery Shopper can "shop" over the phone to check your Customer Service Representative's performance.

Mystery Shoppers work undercover, so they look and sound like regular customers.

They pay attention to the Sales Process and make note of your team's performance. The Mystery Shopper may return an item to test how well your team responds. The Mystery Shopper will submit a written report on his or her experience. Take a look at the sample Customer Service Representative Mystery Shop Report in this book. Download a customizable copy; order The Complete Suite from the Buy Stuff page at www.barebonesbiz.com.

You could make arrangements with a friend who owns a non-competing company to Mystery Shop each other's businesses. Put together checklists to help standardize the performance assessments.

Mystery Shopping Services

At what point does it make sense to use a professional service? According to Linda Prayer of National Shopping Service, "A professional service will give you more objective results." Also, hiring a professional Mystery Shopping service makes sure that you actually follow through on the program. Check out National Shopping Service at www.nationalshoppingservice.com. Or call 800.800.2704.

Basic Mystery Shopping Guidelines

- Plan your Mystery Shopping program before you launch it.
- Announce the program to your team and explain the procedures in detail. Let them know that Mystery Shoppers will be stopping by or calling for service. When and where will be a surprise!
- Expect some pushback. "You don't trust me," is the underlying concern. Approach Mystery Shop ping as a way to help your team members improve their performance. If you are serious about creating excellence in your company, this can be a transformational tool.
- Make a game of it...and reward good perfor mance generously! Celebrate success and dust yourselves off when you fall down. The Goal is constant improvement in the delivery of your USP.

Circulate Among the Troops Exercise

Today, spend an hour on the floor or in the field. Interact with your customers. Ask them about what they need and want ...and listen to their answers. Notice whether your USP is being delivered in every transaction. Observe your company as if you were a customer. Is it clean, professional and friendly? Are you fulfilling your promises to your customers?

Are your team members willingly using your Procedures? Are your Procedures helping make good sales, or do they need revamping? Notice who is doing a great job and acknowledge them for it. Notice non-compliance and pull the offending team member aside and address it privately. Pitch in and help when help is needed.

Show your customers and your employees how passionate you are about your Mission. Let them know you are on the lookout for better ways to serve your customers.

Look, listen and learn. Clarity lights the path to greatness.

Sample Document Mystery Shopping Scorecard

Customer Service Representative CSR

Date __________

CSR Name_________________________

Mystery call made by________________

Your call was answered promptly YES NO

If no, please explain: ________________________________ ______________________

The CSR answered the phone in a pleasant voice. YES NO

The CSR used the approved greeting. YES NO

The CSR asked for your contact information. YES NO

The CSR was polite and willing to help. YES NO

The CSR explained the service fee. YES NO

The CSR attempted to schedule the service call. YES NO

Overall score of the phone call: 1 2 3 4 5 (1 is POOR and 5 is EXCELLENT)

Day 27 TUESDAY'S COACHING LESSON: MAKING IT RIGHT

"When you lay an egg, stand back and admire it!"
~ Dale Carnegie

You are building your company with the best intentions. You are pursuing a lofty Mission. You are working passionately and tirelessly to create a company that dazzles your customers with wonderful products and services. You are building Procedures to deliver your USP consistently. You are training your team to do the right things.

Still…at some point, you are going to blow it.

And when you blow it, you may hear about it. At some point Ted, the owner of See More Blinds, Inc., may hear…

"Your installer tracked mud on my carpet!"

"The blinds are the wrong color!"

"You ripped me off. My brother-in-law has a friend who knows a guy who can install blinds for half of the money I paid you."

Responding to a customer complaint is a Quadrant I activity…urgent and important. For every problem, real or imagined, I suggest this strategy for making it right…

Let your customer know that you are concerned!

Assure him that you will do whatever it takes to make the situation right.

Ask her what she wants you to do to make it right.

Do that…and a little bit more. Aim to astonish him with your more-than-asked-for response.

Admit it when you've messed up. Apologize and make it right. Bless your complaining customers! You can make it right with them and use the experience to improve your business. The customers who are upset but don't complain will just take their business elsewhere…and you will never know. Too much of that will sink your business. (Hence, the Coaching Lesson for Day 26!)

Sometimes a customer will complain because he or she intends to rip you off and try to get something for nothing. Has that ever happened to you?

Sure, you can make a big deal about who is right and who is wrong. The truth is, 98% of people are trying to do the right things. Just 2% of people, well, they are just nasty people. Don't fuss over the 2%. Focus on the 98%. Save yourself some grief and aggravation. Cut to the chase. Find out what your customer wants you to do…and do it.

Should you receive a price complaint, try this approach:

"Mr. Fernwicky, I wish it were not so expensive to run a professional plumbing company. The trucks, the insurance, the training, the inventory, the safety programs, the 24-hour phone service, the wages for top-notch plumbers…it costs a lot to put this show on the road. Our prices are based on our costs of doing business. Our prices are fair, and we try to provide great service. "

"However, in this instance, we have failed to communicate the value of that service to you and for that, I apologize."

"Our goal is your 100% satisfaction. What's it going to take to make you 100% satisfied with our service?"

Listen. Then do it. Plus a little bit more. This approach will avoid lots of wrinkles and gray hair.

"The weak can never forgive. Forgiveness is the attribute of the strong."
~ Mahatma Gandhi

Make it Safe to Serve.

Let your employees know that mistakes are bound to happen. Their response to a mistake can be your company's shining moment. Stick with a problem until it is resolved, and you can turn an angry customer into a raving fan.

Make it clear to your employees that they won't ever get in trouble for attempting to solve a problem for a customer. Let them know that Procedures should support good sales and service, not hinder their efforts to make customers happy. Service to customers is Job One. Revamp Procedures that are getting in the way of sales.

"I tell my team that I will support any and all efforts to serve our customers. You just cannot lose when your motivation is to be of service."

~ Courtney McKenna Gibbs, Nordstrom Store Manager

What Mama Taught You

Most customer service problems stem from poor manners. Remember what your mama taught you about manners? Good manners are the little things that we do for each other to grease the skids of communication.

Here's what mama teaches…

- Say "please" and "thank you." Even to family members.
- Don't yell at people.

Create a Proactive Publicity Procedure

What would you do if you learned that the investigative TV show "48 Hours" just filmed your employee on a service call at Mr. Fernwicky's house? The correct answer is to activate your already-written Publicity Procedure. Learn how publicity works. A fascinating book on the subject is High Visibility, by Rein, Kotler and Stoller. The best defense is a good offense. Discover Dean Rotbart, a Pulitzer Prize-nominated journalist who helps business owners build more effective relationships with the media. Meet Dean and sign up for one of his workshops at www.newsbios.com. Have a Procedure in place for both positive and negative media attention. Work out a Procedure for getting media attention for all the wonderful work that you do. Send press releases to the local TV and radio stations announcing employee accomplishments, charitable events and timely public-interest information. Keep your website current and loaded with valuable and helpful information regarding your industry. Do what it takes to make it right. Resolve the situation…and turn it into your shining hour.

- No hitting.
- Monitor your personal noises, including but not limited to…coughing, throat clearing, sniffling, knuckle cracking, gum popping, eardrum equalizing…you know the others. No swearing.
- Criticize in private.
- Praise in public and praise in private…Catch people doing things right all day. It's good manners.
- Don't interrupt.
- Listen.
- Introduce people.
- Offer whatever it is you are offering to your guests first.
- Send thank-you notes and/or gifts. Handwritten notes get bonus points.
- Give genuine compliments. Comment on nice manners.
- Ask permission to place someone on hold on the telephone.
- When you are wrong, say you're sorry.

Help the people on your team learn manners by your good example. Maybe their mamas didn't teach them.

Say You're Sorry Exercise

Today, spend some time reflecting on your relationships. Have you fallen out of touch with a customer, friend or family member over some miscommunication or unresolved problem?

Today you are going to settle the upset. Forgive him or her. Forgive yourself. Knock the chip off your shoulder. Life is too short to create unnecessary boundaries.

Call and say you're sorry.

Day 28 WEDNESDAY'S COACHING LESSON: SUPER-THINKING

"The greatest pleasure in life is doing what people say you can't do."
~ Walter Bagehot

At Bare Bones Biz, Inc., we love problems! A problem is the fertile soil from which opportunity grows. If your customers didn't have problems, they wouldn't call you.

Say it out loud: "I LOVE PROBLEMS!"

Sometimes we just get stuck. The problem with a problem is that you don't know what to do to turn it into an opportunity. Then the problem starts to gnaw at you. A problem can cause you to worry, and worrying is not good for your health!

Today, you'll learn a powerful brainstorming exercise: Super-Thinking! This Procedure will help you solve problems, get focused, banish worry and discover opportunity.

Super-Thinking is based on the classic work of Dale Carnegie. In his book How To Stop Worrying and Start Living, he says:

> *Experience has proved to me, time after time, the enormous value of arriving at a decision. I found that fifty percent of my worries vanish once I arrive at a clear, definite decision; and another forty percent vanish once I start to carry out that decision. So I banish ninety percent of worry by taking these four steps:*
>
> - *Writing down precisely what I am worrying about.*
> - *Writing down what I can do about it.*
> - *Deciding what to do.*
> - *Starting immediately to carry out that decision.*

Our version of Super-Thinking goes like this...

1. Write down precisely what the problem or challenge is.
2. Write down at least 20 ideas of what might be done about it.
3. Decide what to do.
4. Start immediately to carry out that decision.

Dale Carnegie keyed into the most powerful component of this process: To solve the problem and banish the worry, you must write it out! The "overwhelm" goes away once we expose thoughts to paper.

"The man who insists upon seeing with perfect clearness before he decides, never decides. Accept life, and you cannot accept regret."
~ Henri Frederic Amiel

The most important element of our Super-Think version is the list of 20 ideas. Not only is there a solution to your problem, you have lots of options. The really creative ideas are going to be numbers 14 through 20!

Then, decide…and start immediately to carry out that decision.

The Super-Thinking exercise can be performed individually or within a group to take advantage of its creativity.

Super-Thinking Exercise

In Week Two, you started your Position Descriptions. At that time, we suggested that you revisit your employee compensation program after you worked with your Budget and assembled actual financial data. You've gathered data from the Scorecards, too, and you have been working on the Procedures. Now you are better prepared to work on your compensation program.

Today's exercise is to have a Super-Thinking meeting with your team to develop a Bonus Procedure. Start the meeting by letting them know that you appreciate them, that you intend to make sure that as the company grows they are justly rewarded. Ask for their help with this challenge…

"How can we reward those who go above and beyond Goals and Performance standards?"

Now go through the steps of the Super-Thinking exercise. Insist that they write down 20 ideas. Then, write all the ideas down on a flip chart or dry-erase board at the front of the room.

Note that business is not a democracy. You want their input. And you may even have the team members vote on their top three favorite ideas. But you will make the final decision. Your team expects you to. They will be pleased that you sought their input. And you will be well served by letting their opinions impact your decision. That will make it easier for team members to "buy in" on the Bonus Procedure.

End the meeting. Review the ideas. Look over your performance Scorecards. Consider the financial impact of the Bonus Program. Adjust your Budget as needed. Then…decide and ACT.

When you unveil the Bonus Procedure, let your team know that you will "test drive" it for 60 days. That way, you can measure performance and financial data and see if the Bonus Procedure is working. If it needs to be changed, you can Super-Think the solution.

Update your Position Descriptions and add the Bonus Procedure to your Plan Binder in the *Building the Team* section.

Super-Thinking will help you make sure you keep moving in the direction of your Mission, Vision and Goals. Use it to help you create Procedures and tackle the projects on your Top Projects List.

Listen to Innovate

Bite your tongue as you list and share your ideas. If you shut down the ideas too quickly, you discourage the team. And why not try something a bit off the wall? You'll learn something.

"Life affords no higher pleasure than that of surmounting difficulties, passing from one step of success to another, forming new wishes and seeing them gratified. He that labors in any great or laudable undertaking has his fatigues first supported by hope and afterward rewarded by joy."

~ Samuel Johnson

Day 29 THURSDAY'S COACHING LESSON: MAKE SURE YOUR BUSINESS IS SERVING YOU

"You can have anything you really, really, really, really want. That's the good news. You will also have anything you really, really, really, really don't want."

~ Dr. Wayne Dyer

Setting Sight Reflection Exercise

Spend an hour today reflecting on the past six weeks. Pull out your Journal and start reading it from the beginning. Isn't it amazing how much you have accomplished? Your business is different from what it was six weeks ago. Certainly, you've changed too.

Reflect on all that you have created. Good for you. I am proud of you. So often we neglect to acknowledge and enjoy our victories because so many battles lie ahead. Today, take a moment to congratulate yourself on your accomplishments. By following this six-week plan, even if you have only done 25% of what I have asked you to do, you have accomplished more than most business owners ever will.

Review your Plan Binder. Flip through each section. As you do, reflect on these questions and write your thoughts and feelings in your Journal...

- What has changed...in yourself, in your business?
- What have you accomplished?
- Is your business consistent with your Mission?
- Is your business accomplishing its Vision?
- Is your business supporting your Values?
- Are you making more money?
- Are you making enough money?
- Are you reaching your Goals?
- Are you having fun?
- Are you making a positive difference in people's lives?
- Are your relationships strong and healthy?
- Are you fit and strong...physically and spiritually?
- Are you moving closer to your Perfect Life?
- If you could shut down your business with a snap of your fingers, would you?

You were wise to invest your time the past six weeks improving yourself and your business. Profitability can make the difference between a business that serves your life and a business that doesn't. Money is terrific, but it is not the only measure of success. Does your business serve your life?

Remember, if your business falls short of your wildest dreams, there are only two possible reasons:

1. You are neglecting to do the Bare-Bones Basics that make all the difference to your success.
2. You are not clear on what you want.

The words of Dr. Wayne Dyer that opened this chapter are a good reminder that we need to be clear about what we want and focus on it. What we focus on, we manifest.

Draw a line down the center of a page in your Journal. Put a minus sign at the top left and a plus sign at the top right. Now list the negatives and positives of your business. This is the classic Ben Franklin method of decision-making. See if the pluses outweigh the minuses.

Should the business stay in your life? Should it go?

My friend Paul Swan adds another element to the decision-making process: "Test drive" the answers in your mind. Pretend you snapped your fingers and made the business go away. How does it feel? Perhaps according to the Ben Franklin test, the minuses outweigh the pluses. If you find yourself feeling deeply disappointed with the logical answer, consider how you can change the minuses into plusses.

Should you keep working your business plan or change your direction...and your business? Essentially, it's a spiritual question. You are exchanging a good portion of your life for your business. It has to serve you and it has to serve others. Search your heart. Meditate. Pray. Ask for peace and guidance.

Many years ago, a friend of mine successfully climbed a 24,000-foot mountain peak. Afterward, he said something that stuck with me. He mentioned that not everyone made it to the top. One of the members of his party struggled with altitude sickness and had to turn around less than 1,000 feet from the summit.

"He must have been hurting pretty bad," I commented.

"Well," my friend responded, "It had better be pretty bad before you turn around. Because once you turn back, the pain goes away. Then you forget how bad it was. And you start to wonder, 'Could I have made it?'"

Now, you may choose to take a different route. Or change your pace... or your climbing partners. Or you might try again after you repair some equipment. But if your Mission represents the summit, if you are clear on what you want, don't give up. Just keep applying the Bare Bones Business Basics. Improve your knowledge and skills in each area of your business. Make decisions and take action. And press on!

And if you choose another path?

Here is a story from a wonderful book called Mastery: The Keys to Success and Long-Term Fulfillment, by George Leonard:

> *When Jigoro Kano, the founder of Judo, was quite old and close to death, the story goes, he called his students around him and told them he wanted to be buried in his white belt. What a touching story; how humble of the world's highest-ranking judoist in his last days to ask for the emblem of the beginner! But Kano's request, I eventually realized, was less humility than realism. At the moment of death, the ultimate transformation, we are all white belts. And if death makes beginners of us, so does life – again and again.*

Today, I make a conscious commitment:

To move forward with my business plan…or choose another path.

I choose…

Signed:______________________ Date:______________

If you choose to commit to move forward with your plan, don't question your decision...for at least six weeks. Give your mind a rest and allow yourself to just be successful.

Day 30 FRIDAY'S COACHING LESSON: TELL YOUR STORY

The Bare Bones Biz Plan will support the decision you made yesterday. The skills you've learned over the past six weeks will help you craft a better life and be useful in all of your business adventures. I am here to help you grow in the direction of your Perfect Life!

You are creating the story of your life with each experience. Today's lesson is about sharing your story.

"Imagining where we want to go, developing a strategic plan, setting goals, communicating the information, executing the plan and measuring our progress gives us a sustainable advantage over our competitors. It starts with imagining."
~ Ernest "J.R." Richardson

The Story of You

Once upon a time, in the late 1970s, there was a young prince named Andy Grove. Andy was the CEO of Intel, Inc. Andy's company had a very focused product line: computer memory chips. Intel was the biggest and best producer of computer memory chips in the world.

But in a land far, far away, Japanese manufacturers were creating their own memory chips. Their chips were faster and less expensive than Intel's chips. Intel tried to hang on to market share by seeking out niche markets for Intel chips and by improving the quality of the products. All to no avail, for Intel's profits and market share continued to dwindle. Shareholders were not happy.

During this crisis, Grove walked into Intel co-founder Gordon Moore's office and asked him a compelling question.

"If we get kicked out and the board brings on a new CEO, what do you think he'd do?"

"He'd probably get us out of memory chips," Moore replied.

"Why shouldn't you and I walk out the door, come back, and do it ourselves?" Grove asked.

They decided to abandon Intel's biggest business - memory - and move into uncharted waters - microprocessors. It was a gutsy move that ultimately saved the company.

And they all lived happily ever after.

Actually, I don't know about happily ever after, but I do know that Intel has more than 80% market share in the microprocessor industry.

Andy Grove uses this story to communicate how Intel has responded to market changes. He uses it to create a change-tolerant culture at his company. Andy could just announce to his employees that they need to adapt easily to change, and the company must take great risks to survive and thrive. He could simply tell his employees he is a great leader. But it works better to tell the story.

Author Noel M. Tichy tells this story about Andy Grove and describes how winning companies create leaders at every level in his terrific book The Leadership Engine. Tichy examines leaders like Grove, Dick Notebart of Ameritech and Jack Welch of General Electric looking for clues as to what makes a great leader. Leaders, he found, develop more leaders. In this way, they create a company that can continue to win. "Six characteristics," Tichy says, "define winning leaders: teaching, learning, ideas, values, energy and edge. The ultimate hallmark of world-class, champion leaders is the ability to weave all the other elements together into vibrant stories that lead their organizations into the future."

Leadership is all about change. It's about getting people to follow you into the unknown. To get people to see the future, first take them there in their imaginations. Tell them a story.

Great leaders tell great stories. Tichy describes three kinds of stories that make up a great leader's storyline. You can learn the elements of these stories to help you develop your own storyline…and your leadership skills.

"Who I Am" stories. These stories explain who you are and how you came to be that way. Often, these are stories from your childhood. Did you have to walk six miles to school each day? Did you drop out of school to run the family business when your dad got sick? Did you marry your high school sweetheart 47 years ago, and do you still hold hands at the movies? These stories illustrate your strengths and values and let folks know what makes you tick. Are you competitive? That can be a powerful leadership trait. Share how you discovered your competitive nature by telling a story about winning the 3A high school wrestling championship.

"Who We Are" Stories. Martin Luther King, Jr., galvanized the Civil Rights Movement by declaring, "If I am stopped, this movement will not stop. Kill me, but know that if you do, you have 50,000 more to kill." Through his speeches, his stories, King created a nation of activists. He made people understand their roles and responsibilities in his dream. Great leaders understand that significant change takes the energy and talent of other people. Tell stories that illustrate how your team fits into the picture.

"Future" Stories. Craft a story that describes your Mission and why you are so passionately heading in that direction. Create a picture of your Vision. Explain what the business looks like…a year from now, two years from now and happily ever after. What are the career and ownership paths in your company? What are the future opportunities for team members to pursue to their highest purposes? What future can you build together? What does your Perfect Life look like?

Tell Your Story Exercise

Today, gather your employees. Tell them your story. As Zig Ziglar says, "Rip open your chest and let them see your heart."

Your Weekend Homework

Take the weekend off. Recharge! Have fun with your family.

Keep your appointment Sunday night or Monday morning. Look over the Bare Bones Biz Maintenance Plan…and get growing!

By the way…remember Ted, the owner of See More Blinds, Inc.? Check out his Perfect Life. He updated it a few days ago.

"Our children may learn about heroes of the past. Our task is to make ourselves architects of the future."

~ Mzee Jomo Kenyatta

Sample Document Ted's Perfect Life

I wake up…At 7:30 am. I take a long walk on the beach, right outside my home. I have breakfast with Anita, my beautiful wife. Eggs and bacon and a perfect piece of pineapple.

I drive to See More Blinds along the Coast Highway in my new Mini Cooper, dark red with grey stripes.

At the office, I do some Managing By Walking Around. I touch base with each team member. At 10 a.m., we meet to go over the Plan Binder and review our actual financial performance and our budgets. Right on target to hit $2 million in sales with 25% growth and profitability.

I interview a candidate for our new sales territory. And I hire her. I tell her my story and I show her my Plan Binder.

After lunch (a cheesesteak from the deli), I work on my Top Projects. We are opening our second location of See More Blinds. The Grand Opening is scheduled for May.

I call my Board of Advisors, just to say hello and see if I can help them in any way. I write a check for $100,000 to the Juvenile Diabetes Association. I look up my financial portfolio on the Internet and note my net worth is $1 million and I am debt-free. I am grateful.

At about 2 p.m., I meet with a smart teenager with a terrific business idea. We look through his Plan Binder and I help him tweak his business plan. I agree to invest $500 to get him started.

I meet with Suki to congratulate her on hitting Goals. We work on our employee stock distribution plan.

arrange a tennis date with our son Max and we agree to meet at 4:30. I call Anita to have her meet us there and bring our daughter, Roxy, so we can play doubles. In the evening, we walk through our gardens and pick fresh vegetables for dinner. We play games and read. I give thanks and pray. I relax …And then I go to sleep.

Going
Forward: The
Maintenance
Plan

The Bare Bones Biz Plan!...Business Body-Building!

Six weeks puts the pressure on…so that you will make great progress in a short time.

Congratulations! You did it!

You have a business plan…you have your Bare Bones Biz Plan Binder. This is not a business plan to be tossed into a file drawer with a dismissive, "There, that's done." The Bare Bones Biz Plan is designed to get your business jump-started and help you keep your business growing and thriving. The basics work…from Main Street to Wall Street…as far as you want to go.

The Maintenance Plan

Keep the good habits you have developed working for you in the weeks to come. Go back to the beginning of this book. And go through this plan again. Spend one week in each section of your business and "plus" the work you did the first time around.

And just like a physical fitness program, as your company gets stronger, you will find that improving each section of your plan takes less time. Your company won't need the attention it needs now as your people become more capable and your systems get simpler and better.

Six weeks of The Bare Bones Biz Plan will transform your business. However, you can benefit from staying on the plan indefinitely. Most importantly, keep your appointment with yourself Sunday night or Monday morning. Continue to ask the big questions. Keep asking and listening. Think. Gather data. Consider your options. Decide on a course of action…and take it.

Here are the basic meetings and reports you need…

Daily

- ☐ Scorecards for each division
- ☐ Review sections of your Plan Binder as needed
- ☐ M.B.W.A. (Managing by Walking Around)

Weekly

- ☐ Financial Quick Check, Income Statement and Balance Sheet
- ☐ Budget updates
- ☐ Marketing Calendar
- ☐ Mystery Shopping Reports

- ☐ Top Projects meetings as needed
- ☐ Individual Performance meetings
- ☐ Sales meeting
- ☐ Sunday night/Monday morning meeting with yourself

Stop by www.barebonesbiz.com to see what's new to help you!

Monthly

- ☐ Month-End Checklist and financial package
- ☐ Divisional meetings
- ☐ May *The Bare Bones Biz Plan* be part of your lifelong self- and business-development program!

Keep coming back...to www.barebonesbiz.com!

My Mission is Worldwide Business Literacy. Thank you for your support and participation. I would love to hear your story.

I decided to deliver this book as a downloadable file so that I could get feedback, suggestions, and ideas from YOU...and regularly update and improve the book and the forms. I am here to serve you and help you start, fix and grow your business.

Share your story. You've put together your Plan Binder. You've spent six weeks creating your Bare Bones Biz Plan. How are you doing? I want to hear from you! Contact me to share your experience. I can include your story in the next edition of the book! Offer suggestions for making it better. What can I do to improve my products and services? I LOVE hearing from you!

Keep checking in at www.barebonesbiz.com. I am here to help you get going and growing with your business!

Special thanks to...

Hot Rod and Max xoxo

Yai, Papu, Lynn, Tae, Gail, Jim, Peggy, Andy, all the Gypsy Kids, Andrea, Shauna, Michelle and Jon, Paul, Al, Dan, Jim, Steve, Katie, Kelly, JR, Keresa, Lisa, Jamie, Marla, Missy, Lisa, Cathy, Mo, Courtney, Dianne, Billy, Bill, Tim, Jo, Ruth, Hal, Christian, Jules, Nancy, Dean, Frank, Harry, John, Jim, Amy, Nick, Pete, Scott, Jim, Steve, Katie, Kelly, Matt, Kim, Lisa, Donald, Matt, Jeff, Lisa, Kelley, Jack, Dan, Mike, Lyn, John and all the Revolutionaries, the Challengers and our beloved Bare Bones Biz Clients...

...and all the others who have helped and inspired me!

About Bare Bones Biz and Author Ellen Rohr

I almost sunk our family business. I assumed I knew enough about business to run a dinky little plumbing company. After all, I had spent about $100,000 of my parents' money on my college degree in Business Administration. In fact, I graduated at the top of my class. Still, I didn't know how to balance a checkbook!

I got involved in my husband's company after his partner died unexpectedly. Boy, was I humbled! It seemed like lots of money was moving through the company, but at the end of the month there was never any money left. Thankfully, I found a mentor, a savvy plumbing contractor. Frank Blau wrote a column in Plumbing & Mechanical magazine. I wrote to him and asked for help. He took me under his wing and taught me how to keep score in business. He taught me how to read and use financial reports. He taught me how to make money.

We turned our company around. We paid off our business loan. We doubled sales and tripled the amount of money we took out of the company. Very cool. My husband and I went middle-age crazy. We sold the company to our employees – a friendly coup d'etat! – and bought a gentleman's farm in the country. (Picture "Green Acres.") At this point, I realized that I wanted to share what I'd learned. After all, if a smart, highly educated person like me didn't know how to read a Balance Sheet, I figured business illiteracy must be rampant. I was right.

My experiences since then have included teaching and consulting with hundreds of small businesses, primarily plumbing and heating companies. In my seminars, I rarely find a student who creates and reads financial statements on a regular basis, much less uses financial information to make management decisions. In fact, few know their assets from their liabilities!

I started Bare Bones Biz – a training and consulting company – to teach folks how to turn their big ideas into successful businesses. I teach the basics, the simple disciplines that can take your company from flab to fit. I've written two books on business basics, *Where Did the Money Go? – Accounting Basics for the Business Owner Who Wants to Get Profitable*, and *How Much Should I Charge? – Pricing Basics for Making Money Doing What You Love.*

My consulting work led to a position as president of Benjamin Franklin Plumbing, a home-service plumbing franchise company. We grew from zero to $40 million in franchise sales, the 18th-fastest growing franchise in 2003. I learned a lot about what works to grow fast and profitably...and what doesn't. Guess what! The basics never go out of style, no matter how big a company gets. (If the accounting gets confusing, then watch out for Tyco- and Enron-esque criminal activity. The buzzword on Wall Street these days is "transparency." That means keeping business systems simple and the financial information clearly available, just as I describe in The Bare Bones Biz Plan.)

Bare Bones Biz is an exciting company. I love my team! We work together to develop books, products, seminars and services designed to help you have more fun and make more money in business.

This book, The Bare Bones Biz Plan, is an essential part of my plan to help improve business literacy. It ties into my website, www.barebonesbiz.com, THE community for BASIC business information.

Together, we can build extraordinary businesses and expand World Peace.

TELL US YOUR BIZ SUCCESS STORY!

The Bare Bones Biz Team
info@barebonesbiz.com
www.barebonesbiz.com
877.629.7647
417.753.3685 fax
3120 S. Know It All Lane
Rogersville, MO 65742

I wish you love, peace and lots of money!

CPSIA information can be obtained at www.ICGtesting.com
Printed in the USA
LVOW030954170412
277948LV00001B/13/P